JOSSY'S GIANTS

'That fellow is a legend, he's Joswell 'Jossy'
Blair and I've read about him in football
books. He was the talk of the North-east
from the age of twelve. He was a fanatic.
Jossy had only one aim in life – to play for
Newcastle United.

'His dream came true. In front of 50,000
chanting fans he ran out on to St James'
Park for his first match in the first team. He
played a blinder but, four minutes from the
end, he was scythed down from behind. A
crack echoed around the stunned stadium!
He never played professional football
again.'

But as far as the Glipton Grasshoppers are
concerned, it'll take more than a crock
Geordie to set them on the road to football
success!

This book is based on the BBC TV series *Jossy's Giants* by Sid Waddell produced by Paul Stone and directed by Edward Pugh. The main characters were played as follows: Jossy Blair, Jim Barclay; Ross Nelson, Mark Gillard; Tracey Gaunt, Julie Foy; Ricky Sweet, Paul Kirkbright; Harvey McGuinn, Julian Walsh.

About the author

Sid Waddell is a Geordie, born in a pit village eighteen miles north of Newcastle-on-Tyne. There football was a part of life: the boys played all day and half of the night – and the ambition of every one of them was to play for Newcastle United.

Sid's career has been in television and he is known to millions as a BBC darts commentator. Married with five children, Sid Waddell lives in Yorkshire.

The idea for JOSSY'S GIANTS came when Sid's son Daniel started to play for Churwell Lions, a boys' team in West Leeds.

JOSSY'S GIANTS

Sid Waddell

BBC/KNIGHT BOOKS.

Copyright © Sid Waddell 1986

First published 1986 by the British Broadcasting Corporation/Knight Books

British Library Cataloguing in Publication Data

Waddell, Sid
  Jossy's giants.
  I. Title
  823′.914[F]   PR6073.A2/

  ISBN 0-340-38727-0

Printed and bound in Great Britain for the British
Broadcasting Corporation, 35 Marylebone High Street,
London W1M 4AA and Hodder and Stoughton
Paperbacks, a division of Hodder and Stoughton Ltd.,
Mill Road, Dunton Green, Sevenoaks, Kent (Editorial
Office: 47 Bedford Square, London WC1B 3DP) by
Richard Clay Ltd., Bungay, Suffolk.

To
Sonny Sweeney,
Barry Thomas
and the Churwell Lions

ONE

Jossy Blair always got restless as three o'clock approached on a Saturday afternoon. It was no time to be stuck in a shop. It was time for the smell of liniment, churned-up mud and grass. It was the time for thousands of Geordie voices to swell the battle cry of 'Howway the lads'. It was the time for the Liverpools, Evertons and Tottenhams to tremble as they ran out on to St James' Park to face the 'Mighty Magpies' – the one and only Newcastle United.

Jossy stopped the heady flow of memory but his adrenalin was still on full tap. He tried to turn his mind to 'business'. In the six hours that 'Magpie Sports' had been open, he had sold one hold-all, two pieces of billiard chalk and four sets of laces for trainers. Near the till were a couple of unopened letters that had arrived earlier. Both, Jossy was sure, contained bills, and one was lettered a very dangerous-looking red. He picked them up and placed them carefully in an old-fashioned attaché case full of other unattended paperwork. For a few seconds he tickled a duster over boxes marked Nike, Adidas and Puma; then the adrenalin beat the business five-nil.

Jossy almost long-jumped across the shop and turned the sign to 'Closed'. In a moment he had shot into the back room and slipped out of his clothes and into trainers, shorts and a black-and-white striped Newcastle

7

United shirt of the early 1970s with a big red number six on the back. Over this he pulled a lurid Newcastle tracksuit top and trousers. As he zipped up the top his eyes strayed to the framed picture hanging above the gas ring. It showed the Newcastle first team in 1971. In the front row, sitting next to the bandy, brilliant legs of 'Supermac' Malcolm McDonald, was a slightly thinner Jossy Blair, glowing with pride. Scrawled across the bottom in a bold hand were the words *To Jossy, a great player and a canny lad. All the best, Supermac.*

The misty look disappeared from Jossy's pale blue eyes. He licked his fingers and patted a few strands of ginger-blond hair down over his scalp, muttering 'Howway the lads' almost as a prayer. After a quick glance in a small mirror above the sink, he turned and left the shop. Soon he was jogging down Church Street in the loose way of an ex-athlete, whistling 'Blaydon Races' for all he was worth.

His path took him through the centre of Glipton, a small mill town just on the Manchester side of the Pennines. The church was made of the same yellowish stone as the square-built houses, some of them with long high windows, where the weavers used to work. Jossy ran past the Chinese chip shop which advertised *Genuine Lancashire Cornish pasties*, a betting shop that he often patronised and turned left at the 'Turk's Head', a pub where he had the odd glass of sweet stout. Then he jogged down what the locals called a ginnel towards the recreation ground by the canal.

A brightly-painted narrow boat was approaching the lock. Jossy stopped to watch and do some toe-touching exercises. The people on board were obviously week-enders, a bit too dressed up, a bit over-jolly. He looked beyond the black-and-white painted boarding around the lock at the swelling moors behind the viaduct. They curled around the town like a sleeping giant. For a moment Jossy thought of the moors and crags of the North Tyne valley; of slag-heaps and pulley-wheels. But that was a dream of 'home'; Glipton was where he lived. He jogged on.

At the far end of the Glipton Municipal Recreation Ground was a tatty no-man's land containing a football pitch laughingly referred to locally as 'Canalside Stadium'. This was mainly thanks to a very rusty corrugated-iron stand, a rickety pavilion-style changing hut, and remnants of a wooden fence around the touch-lines. The place had once been the pride of the Fartown Falcons, a local mill football team, but they had long since flown, and now the ground was home to a boys' team, the Glipton Grasshoppers, whose playing record just about matched their surroundings. It was abysmal.

Manager Albert Hanson, whose face normally had the expression of a hungry bloodhound, was too sick to even shout as his team of twelve-year-olds came ever more, in football terms, 'under the cosh'. It was half-way through the first half and already the Tatton Thunderbirds, a big confident bunch in bright red strips, were one goal up. As their attack once more cut through the Grasshoppers' defence like an Exocet missile through confetti, Albert deserted his post on the touch-line. Too scared to watch any more, he stepped behind a gnarled old oak tree at the end of the ground.

Nobody on the pitch noticed. Ricky Sweet, a dour-faced low-browed boy, was the captain and was doing his best. But even he could not stem the tide or stop his other defenders from sprawling about the pitch like palsied seals. As the Thunderbird centre-forward doddled through to face goalie Harvey McGuinn, Ricky, whose passion for computers had taught him crisp, precise use of English, said what many were thinking; 'Rubbish. That's what we are. Rubbish.'

None of the sprawlers in yellow shirts or the gaggle of loyal parents on the touch-line would have disagreed at that moment. In fact Tracey Gaunt, the fourteen-year-old bucket person to the team, was thinking that they were all running about like a bunch of headless chickens, but she kept her opinions to herself. Albert was still hiding behind the tree so it was up to Tracey to offer the firm opinion of sound strategy: 'Close him down, Harvey. Come out – quick. Give him less to shoot at!'

Harvey McGuinn, who was built on the lines of a stick insect, rarely heeded advice – good, bad or otherwise. He really wanted to be an ice dancer and his behaviour in goal often showed this. Now he was prancing, pirouetting and screaming at the Thunderbird centre-forward: 'OK, big man. You've beaten me once, but I've got you worked out this time. It's going to my left!'

The centre-forward, who would have been a Simon le Bon lookalike if he had not been cross-eyed, stopped dead and began foot-juggling the ball. He stared in a highly sarcastic fashion at Harvey's green goalie jersey – under which there was a string vest, a Madness T-shirt and a body warmer – and said loud enough for the rest of the Thunderbirds to hear: 'Hey up, lads. Just cop Michelin Man here. He's trying to talk me off.'

He flipped the ball arrogantly from foot to foot, lobbed it high with his left foot, turned his back to the goal and back-heeled the ball on the volley past Harvey's despairing fingers. As the Thunderbirds did their ritual dance of triumph, Ricky picked the ball from the back of the net and booted it away savagely.

'That's it,' Ricky rasped, mainly to himself. 'If this goes on for the rest of the game, I'm packing up.'

Still flopped on the ground, Harvey raised his head and pointed to a large shiny white Mercedes rolling along the gravel path towards the ground. He raised a gloved hand in pathetic appeal to Ricky: 'We might not get hammered so often if we all turned up at the same time.'

They both watched as a small, dark-haired boy in a very flash, new-looking tracksuit jumped out of the Mercedes and raced towards the pitch. A man in a camel coat got out of the car, stopped to light an enormous Havana cigar and then began a leisurely walk towards the action. Albert, who had obviously noticed the new arrivals, had left his hiding place behind the tree and was waiting for the boy at the half-way line. He was not amused.

'Nice of you to honour us with your company Ross.' The boy was eagerly fastening the laces on his football boots. 'We're half an hour into the first half, we're getting a 2-0 roasting off the Thunderbirds, and you and your dad swan up like Little and Large making a guest appearance!'

Ross Nelson rarely took notice of rockets like this. He *knew* he was the star of the Glipton Grasshoppers. 'My dad had a rush of punters on the three o'clock race. I had to help him.' In a second Ross had his tracksuit off and was running on to the field stuffing his shinpads into his socks. Albert shook his head but the spark of his interest had been rekindled. 'Run at them, Ross. Pressurise them!'

Bob Nelson had heard every word of this but gave nothing away, as usual. He was the local bookie and most of the Grasshoppers' funds for kit, balls, and so on, came from him. His macho moustache twitched as he grinned an oily grin at Albert and offered him a cigar. Albert waved it away and set off on a nervous prowl along the touch-line towards Tracey. Bob blew out a smoke ring and then began 'living' the game: 'Get stuck into them, Ross. Skin him! Heads up the rest of you. Put a *name* on that ball. Make it yours.'

The Grasshoppers needed a lot more than hot air. As

half-time approached, things went from bad to worse. Ross ran about like a clockwork road-runner, tripping over the ball and spending more time on his back than on his feet. The rest of the 'attack' was not exactly on the ball either. Glenn Rix, today sporting a bright red (Manchester United) Mohican hairdo, and Ian 'Selly' Sellick, whose flowing hair was streaked light-blue (Manchester City) were supposed to be twin strikers. Alas, both were besotted with the charms of Tracey Gaunt so they rarely worked as a combined unit! Now they both ogled her like moonstruck calves as she stood behind Harvey's goal trying to calm the lads down.

'Harvey, don't stay on your line all the time. *Read* the play. Ross, move out on to the flanks. Give us width.'

There was no trace of panic in Tracey's voice. All the Grasshoppers knew that she was red hot on football knowledge. Until about a year before, Tracey had joined them in all their playground kickabouts at school. Now she could only watch as the Thunderbirds swarmed towards the Grasshoppers' goal. Ricky was getting through the work like a Trojan but a lovely through ball left even him stranded. Once more Harvey did his impersonation of an electrocuted jack-in-the-box. This time the centre-forward walked the ball round him and rolled it into the net. 3-0. The whistle went for half-time.

The Grasshoppers and their hangers-on mooched over towards Albert and Tracey and the backbiting started, as usual.

'Sorry Albert. I've got other things on my plate. I've had enough.' Harvey McGinn stuck out his non-existent chin and began pulling on his tracksuit top.

Normally this attitude would have raised a few jeers from the rest of the Grasshoppers but today it just about summed up the general mood. Only Ricky Sweet showed any of the normal jokey spirit. 'If you spent half the time thinking about football that you do thinking about that cissy ice-dancing, we might get somewhere.'

Harvey was quick to divert the flak. He glowered at Ross who had his nose in a segment of orange and was keeping a very low profile. Harvey waggled a gloved finger at him: 'Some use to the team you are, showing up half an hour late. Mum pressing your new tracksuit, was she?'

Ross threw down the piece of orange and pounced at Harvey's throat. Albert, almost in tears, stepped between them and held their writhing bodies at arms' length.

'Look you two, and the lot of you. There'll be no thumping while I'm manager of this team. Let's face it, we're playing terrible.' A pale grin flickered across his face. 'But last week the Vikings were 5-0 up on us and we still drew . . .'

'Only 'cos Mr Nelson took over the whistle when the referee jiggered his hamstring.' Ricky was a realist.

Bob Nelson had been listening to this, stroking his moustache thoughtfully and fiddling with his battery of assorted gold rings. He decided to raise morale – in his usual way. With a loud stage cough he opened the boot of his car and produced cans of Coke and Fanta, bags of crisps and every sort of packaged nut you could imagine. The boys began guzzling, crunching and nibbling with gusto, not so much because they were greedy but mainly to avoid any more of the inquest. The diversion did not please Albert.

'What's the sense in filling them up with that lot when there's another half to play?'

Bob favoured him with the kind of grin he usually saved for the mug punters at his betting shop. 'Albert, old son, have you never heard of incentives? Canalside Stadium? Wembley Stadium?. It doesn't matter. All footballers are alike. They need targets.' He turned back to the boys. 'Right, you lot. Go out there and take this lot to the cleaners. I'll play each goal scorer 50 pence. And if we get FIVE goals, I'll take you all to Burger Barneys for hamburger, chips, salad, relish, the works.'

One or two faces showed renewed zest for the contest.

Unknown to the Glipton Grasshoppers, their officials and hangers-on, Jossy Blair had been watching these events from behind a hedge. He had not been impressed. In fact more than once he had been forced to muffle his mouth with his hand to stop laughing out loud. Seeing that the half-time 'junket' was in progress, Jossy began jogging towards the group, eager to get a closer look at these comedians.

One or two of the bunch, including Tracey Gaunt, noticed Jossy. Slightly embarrassed, Jossy began to jog backwards, like footballers often do to work out the muscles down the backs of the legs, and began to sing 'Blaydon Races':

> 'Oh me lads, you shudda' seen we gannin',
> Passin' the folks along the road,
> Just as they were stannin',
> Aal the lads and lasses there,
> Aal wi' smilin' faces
> Gannin' alang the Scotswood Road,
> To see the Blaydon Races.'

By now all the Grasshoppers were looking at him. He stopped level with the group and began doing toe touches. Slowly he raised his head and looked at them, paying particular attention to the eating and drinking. 'Football teams train on pop and crisps down here, do they?' Bob Nelson looked daggers at Jossy, but said nothing. 'I've been watching your antics for the past twenty minutes. Want my honest opinion?'

14

Bob continued to bristle but Albert was all ears. 'Yes Geordie, another helping of criticism isn't going to do any more harm. Fire away.'

Jossy walked lazily around the group like a horse dealer weighing up a possible buy. He stopped beside Harvey. 'Any goalie who uses his mouth more than his gloves is a duck egg.'

One or two of the other boys smiled at this. Harvey began to splutter a protest. Jossy poked at his bulbous jersey. 'I'd tell your mum to stop putting so much self-raising flour in her cakes, too.'

Harvey could only mumble something about wrapping up because he caught cold easily. The grin swiftly left Ross's face as Jossy turned on him. 'You're about as much use to the team as a passing cross-country runner. You never get involved! And why do you keep taking your eye off the ball?'

Ross went red and stared at the ground. His dad looked as though he wanted to muscle in, but the close attention everyone was paying to the Geordie stopped him. As Jossy turned his gaze to Glenn and Selly, a sudden change came over Ross. From being very annoyed he began looking at Jossy with something approaching awe.

Jossy was looking at Glenn and Selly with their colourful hair styles. 'Now I was under the impression that twin strikers would occasionally HEAD the ball. Or would that ruin the styling? If I were the boss round here I'd start a Safari Park, not a football team.' Albert nodded.

Jossy began his jogging. As he moved from them he threw one last thought over his shoulder: 'I hope you've improved a bit by the next time I see you. So long.'

Bob Nelson let out the steam that had been building up. His eyes blazed and his moustache bristled. 'Loud-mouthed Geordies! They're all the same. They come into my shop and they can't simply place a bet. They start the rabbit. They go on about Jackie Milburn this, Kevin Keegan that. They won the Cup donkeys' years ago but they still go on about it. Their brown ale is the greatest, they say, so are their leeks! They get right up my nose.'

Albert did not take too much notice of this outburst. He usually took a good while to make up his mind about things. He spoke carefully: 'Newcastle United are the heirs to a great tradition. Their supporters are real fanatics. And that bloke spoke a lot of sense. He knows his football.'

'He should do. He could have been the greatest!' Ross's words shocked them all. They looked at him, even Harvey, whose imagination had been miles away swirling to the strains of the 'Bolero'.

Ross continued in hushed tones. 'That fellow is a legend. He's Joswell – "Jossy" – Blair and I've read about him in football books.' Ross paused, sensing that he had an eager audience. 'He was the talk of the North-east from the age of twelve. He used to practise for hours in the back lane kicking a tennis ball against the coalhouse door.' Ross was really making a meal of the yarn. 'His mother used to bring out great slices of bread and jam, and he had Tizer and chewing gum to help him concentrate. He was a fanatic. Scouts came from all over the country to the pit village of East Slackburn just to see him.'

Ross sucked on an orange segment for a moment then continued the saga. 'Jossy had only one aim in life – to play for Newcastle United. He got a sackful of England caps as a schoolboy and as a youth. Then on a November day in 1971 Jossy Blair's dream came true. In front of 50,000 chanting fans he ran out on to St James' Park for his first match in the first team. He was twenty and he played at left half.'

'What's that?' asked Harvey.

'Mid-field,' said Albert.

Ross looked round briefly and saw that they were all hanging on to his words, even his dad and Tracey. 'Blair played a blinder. His passing was radar-controlled. But . . . four minutes from the end of the game he was scythed down from behind. A crack echoed around the stunned stadium! He was carried off the park. He never played professional football again.'

Ricky was almost in tears. But Harvey was not impressed. 'Oh, the Geordie's a crock is he? He'd fit in well with us, then.'

The referee's whistle broke the spell and with sighs the lads trotted back to face the second half against the Thunderbirds. Ross hung back thoughtfully and spoke to Tracey.

'It was said at the time that Jossy Blair would make a great manager. But he seemed deliberately to turn his back on the game.'

Tracey looked very serious. 'Then he could be just the person to help us.'

Ross began running towards the action. He shouted back to her, 'Put your thinking cap on, girl. The ship is almost on the rocks. We need a pilot.'

Tracey put her bucket on the ground and sat down on it, her brow creased in thought.

TWO

Tracey Gaunt was not the sort of girl who did her homework with the television on. She was as much a fan of 'Top of the Pops' and 'Emmerdale Farm' as anyone but she always went to her bedroom to hit the books. On the evening after the Grasshopper's latest football disaster she had the house to herself. Her mum and dad had sloped off to the Clough Hall Golf Club and would be happy enough for a couple of hours. Her mum had a nifty line in new golf hats and her dad was never short of a joke for the nineteenth hole. Tracey had a lot of time for both of them but they did not always appreciate her involvement with the Glipton Grasshoppers. Nor, it must be said, did Tracey.

By strong discipline she turned her efforts to English history for an hour. It was a subject she liked and when she packed her books away she felt she had learned something. Then she turned her mind back to the Glipton Grasshoppers in general, and Jossy Blair, the Geordie, in particular. There was no doubt that the team was on the verge of collapse. But how could so apparently flippant a fellow as Blair be persuaded to throw in his lot with them and help them revive?

Ross Nelson had been trying to puzzle out the same thing. Now he was at the youth club sucking a can of Coke and waiting for Tracey. He had thought of taking his dad's advice on the matter but had not bothered.

His dad had obviously not taken to Jossy Blair and, anyway, his dad would probably have suggested something as cynical as out-and-out bribery. 'For £100 I can make you the Brian Clough of Glipton.' Ross shuddered at the thought. Sometimes his dad got on his wires.

Ross looked up as Tracey came in the door. For a moment she looked round with that slightly frightened look that hid the toughness underneath. At one time Ross had fancied Tracey a wee bit but now they were just good buddies. She came over, sat down and refused a drink. 'Had any bright ideas?' she asked.

'Try this one for size.' Ross sat forward eagerly. 'What we need is a bit of inspiration. He is obviously a man who missed out on life, that Geordie. So we persuade him to become our figurehead. We do the business on the pitch and he gets to share the glory.'

Ross beamed at this but Tracey's frown had deepened as he talked. 'You don't seem to agree,' said Ross huffily.

'*You* seem to be forgetting that it's not that often that you lot are any good on the pitch.' Ross started, but said nothing. Tracey continued. 'I agree that Jossy Blair should be the man for us. But I think we've got to take him by surprise. Work a bit of a flanker. Then make him feel he's *wanted*. To me he has the air of a loner, but I'm not sure that's what he wants to be.'

Ross narrowed his eyes. 'What should we do then? Come down his chimney like Santa Claus?'

'No,' replied Tracey quickly. 'As they say in the Westerns – we'll head him off at the pass.'

This left Ross really flummoxed.

Jossy opened his umpteenth tin of beans. He emptied the contents into a pan and started making toast. The waste bin was chokka with bean tins. He made a vow to have salads – tuna, ham, cheese – next week. Half an hour later he had finished his tea and was on the sports pages of *The Journal*, the Newcastle daily paper that his mother sent him. Avidly he devoured the latest about United; he even read through the rugby reports (Daft game, he thought). It was only just after six o'clock so he slipped into his tracksuit and set off for a jog along by the canal.

He was level with a big clump of gorse bushes when he got a surprise. Tracey Gaunt walked out from the bushes and stopped dead in the middle of his tracks. Jossy stopped running but continued exercising on the spot. At first he thought from the look in the girl's eyes that she was upset about something.

'Meeting your boyfriend are you pet? Always late, fella's.'

Tracey looked him straight in the eyes. 'No, Mr Blair. The only fella I'm waiting for is you.'

Jossy was convinced that it was some kind of game. He stopped the exercises and moved closer to the girl. There was something familiar about her. He soon twigged. 'I know you. You're the bucket lassie for that kids' football team. The Grasshoppers is it?. How are they doing?'

'Not very well,' admitted Tracey.

'I've seen more life in a tramp's vest.' Tracey sensed what she thought was more than casual interest. Jossy went on: 'One or two of them are not bad. They need organising.'

Tracey jumped in: 'You're dead right, Mr Blair. They need a strong, forthright, not to say bossy, character to get them together.' She shut up when she saw Jossy was taking the bait.

'What's wrong with the manager you've got now?'

Tracey spoke slowly. 'Oh, Albert's a nice enough man. But he lacks a bit of authority and drive and . . .'

'X-ray eyes,' said Jossy, his eyes narrowing in suspicion. He was looking intently at the bush by the side of the canal towpath. Suddenly he leapt over and parted a section of the bush. In the gap Ross's slightly flushed face appeared.

'Fancy meeting you here,' said Jossy, losing the strong Geordie twang from his voice for a moment. He turned to Tracey and said mockingly in the same voice, 'Oh please come and be our manager Mr Blair. Oh please!'

Jossy began jogging away from them. He shouted back over his shoulder: 'You'll have to think up a better act if you're going to get a saviour for your Grasshoppers. 'Bye.'

Ross patted Tracey gently on the shoulder. 'Nice try, love. But so much for the calm, sensible approach.'

'So what are you going to try?'

Ross pondered, then said softly, 'I'm not quite sure. But take it from me girl, there's more than one way to tickle a trout.'

In the gymnasium of the Glipton Community Centre Albert Hanson was looking at his watch and fretting. He had called a special Grasshoppers' training session for seven o'clock and it was now ten past but there was no sign of any of his team. He began pacing the 5-a-side pitch and booting balls into the net. He grumbled gently to himself.

'I said seven prompt and look what happens. There's no discipline, enthusiasm – nothing in this club. If ever a team needed hard work in training, ours does. I want kids hungry for the game . . .'

An enormous half–pound hamburger, dripping with a rainbow swirl of dressings, burst through the doors with Harvey McGuinn on one end of it. He strode over to the goal-post, leaned casually on it and 'explained' his late arrival. 'Telly was great, Albert. I got so hooked I didn't have time for my tea.'

Albert spoke through clenched teeth. 'I see you're making up for it now.'

The next arrival was a picture of elegance. Ross Nelson was wearing yet another new tracksuit. His trainers shone in a blaze of purple suede and pink rubber. His head was stuck inside the fashion section of a pop magazine. Casually he flipped a page over and showed Albert a picture of a boy modelling leisure clothes. 'You know Albert, French kids think nowt of paying thirty quid for a lambswool tennis shirt with a cobra on the pocket. Good gear, isn't it?'

'If you like that sort of thing,' sighed Albert. He was obviously about to blow a fuse but calmed himself down. 'Right, seeing as you're both here you can start the training.'

Ross looked up from his magazine. 'You can't be serious! Only the *two* of us. Call that training?'

This lit Albert's blue touch paper. He was just sucking in breath to give vent to his feelings when, with a scream of tyres, Selly shot in on a BMX bike. Albert leapt out of the way as Selly launched into a wheelie, mis-cued and landed awkwardly in a heap.

'My leg, my leg,' whined Selly.

He shut up sharpish when he saw the look on Albert's face. Ross and Harvey also caught the mood. The rage had gone out of Albert now. In its place was a weariness that was new to them.

'In the past few weeks we've been duffed up by every team in the League.' Albert's voice was low but each word carried. 'But you lot act as though you're plugged into everything but football.' Harvey scrambled the last of his hamburger into his mouth and Ross tucked the magazine into his tracksuit top. 'I think it's time to pack in.' The boys were all too sick to look at him. 'I admit that I am not the best football manager in the world. Despite what you might reckon, nor are you the best players. We've tried to get some good results. We have failed. I personally move that the Glipton Grasshoppers be disbanded.'

Ross looked up from an intense inspection of the floorboards. 'We could try, Albert. Honest! I know we fool around a bit, but . . .'

Ross's words were interrupted by the flamboyant entrance of his father into the action. Bob was well used to taking the temperature of business meetings and he immediately sensed the need for a boost to morale. His tone was Yorkshire brash. 'What do I see here – a wake? Aren't you excited about my new scheme?'

His words fell on stony ground. Bob was always coming up with schemes and they were usually designed to help one person – Bob.

'Wait till you hear this.' He paused for effect. 'In a few weeks' time it's the finals of the Crampton Cup 5-a-side. If our lot make the final I'm going to buy a full new set of strips.' He looked round for appreciation, enthusiasm, anything. He got none. A note of desperation crept into his delivery. 'I don't know what's the matter with you lot. Look, I don't want even a WIN in the final – though it would be nice. All I want is the team to get there. I'll even give a special trophy to the top scorer.'

Bob's voice tailed away as he said his punchline. Nobody was impressed. He took out a cigar and made a performance of lighting it up. Albert took his whistle off. Carefully he wrapped the string round the whistle and began walking towards the door of the gym. He opened the door, glanced back at the lads and Bob, and made to leave.

A babble of excited female voices washed in from the corridor and the same tide swept Jossy Blair, backwards, almost into Albert's arms. The boys' faces perked up. Jossy's Geordie voice came over half-friendly, half-mocking.

'I'm sorry to burst in on you like this, Grasshoppers and, er, gents. Look, you're a reasonable bunch of lads, I'm needing a bit of a favour. I'm in charge of this bunch of keep-fit lassies who are booked in at eight. But you know what women are like – busy, busy – they've showed up far too early.' He looked round at them and saw that the boys at least were giving him maximum attention. 'You couldn't do me a favour and wind up your training now, could you? You see, if I ask them to hang about, some of them will slope off. That would lose me a few quid . . .' Ross looked at Jossy hard. Jossy tried to backtrack. 'Not that I need the money. I like to do my bit for the local community.'

'We were just packing in anyway,' murmured Albert as he went out. Harvey and Selly mooched past Jossy. Bob Nelson breezed out. Ross took his time.

'What's got into you lot? You look sick as parrots,' said Jossy.

'Parrots are wild with mirth compared with us lot. See you.' Ross left.

Jossy shrugged and turned to his chattering class of ladies. 'OK, lasses. Come on in and let's start getting into shape.'

Soon, to the strain of John Travolta, Jossy was making ten ladies reach to parts that they normally never reached to. He didn't give the Glipton Grasshoppers another thought.

A couple of days later Jossy was hard at work in his sports shop. Trade was at an all-time low so he had decided to have a sale. He was putting the finishing touches to a hand-written poster announcing 'Bargins' when Tracey Gaunt made her entrance.

Jossy eyed her wearily. 'Now I'm a very busy fella, miss. So I want no more nagging sessions about getting going with the Grasshoppers.'

'I think there's an extra "A" somewhere in bargain, Mr Blair.' Tracey said mildly. 'And don't you think it's a rather down-market phrase? I think "Blair's for Better Value" would be much more appropriate!'

Jossy looked at her coolly and slowly and deliberately tore up his notice. Tracey picked up a clean piece of card, sat down at the counter, and began lettering in a neat italic style. Jossy was impressed.

'Hey, you're a dab hand at that, pet.' He paused, then said quietly, 'I'm sorry your team is going through a bad time.'

Tracey said nothing. The doorbell rang and Jossy turned to attend a small male customer who had entered in search of a pair of football boots. After showing the boy the full range, and suspecting he did not have the money to buy a pair anyway, Jossy rejoined Tracey. She was making a fine job of his sign. Then with a start he headed for the door of the shop. Tracey looked up.

'Er, bit of business to attend to, pet. Mind the premises a tick, will you?'

The 'bit of business' was preparing to go over the sticks at Cheltenham and Jossy was off to have a flutter.

The shop doorbell clanged again. Tracey looked up and was surprised to see Glenn and Selly come in. They were equally surprised to see her. Both of the boys did their 'moonstruck calf' act as they passed Tracey. She found them about as attractive as volcanic acne, but she smiled and buckled to her task.

Selly led the way to the boot racks the boy was inspecting. Glenn followed and took a battered old trainer out of his leather jacket. They fell on the kid like a pair of technicolour vultures. He started back, alarmed at their punk gear. He thought he was in for a mugging.

Glenn pushed the trainer at the kid. 'What's your name, sonny?'

'Garth,' said the kid, eyes rolling.

'Well Garth,' Glenn's tone was confiding, 'we are going to give you a bit of good advice.'

'Yeah,' chipped in Selly, spiked hair bristling. 'This fella' Blair is a con-artist.'

The kid's eyes rolled wider. Both the punk Grasshoppers were bending over him now. Glenn tapped the trainer. 'First time I kicked a ball in this, the sole came away.' He showed the damage.

'Why didn't you return them and get your money back?' Garth was on the ball, even when scared. Glenn was stuck for an answer. Selly was deep in thought. Neither noticed that Jossy Blair had slipped in through the rear door. He was earwigging on their conversation. Selly was in full flow.

'When my mate here saw Blair in the street and mentioned the duff trainer, Blair threatened to smack his ear. I'm telling you kid, if your boots are the wrong size, Blair won't change them. He's a right villain.'

Jossy had moved near enough to hear this lot. He tapped Selly on the shoulder and all three boys looked round at him.

'Villain, am I? Trying to put off my potential customers?' Jossy suddenly narrowed his eyes. 'Oh, now I see it all! Boycott my trade. Put me in a hole. Then – IF I become manager of the Grasshoppers – there'll be a deluge of junior sportsmen to ":Magpie Sports". The Al Capone protection racket touch, is it?'

Tracey joined them, tut-tutting and shaking her head. 'I'm afraid that subtlety is not their strong point, Mr Blair. A man of your character . . .'

Jossy butted in. 'I can't quite work out your angle either, sweetheart.' He sounded confused and slightly hurt.

Glenn, Selly and the kid left. Tracey was deeply serious. 'I called in here as an act of friendship, Mr Blair.'

'Jossy, pet.' His tone was gentler.

Tracey scanned the slightly tatty shop. There was dust in some places where there shouldn't be dust. Trade was certainly not booming. She noticed a small brown suitcase beside the till. There were bits of what looked like bills sticking out of it. Jossy noticed her interest. He rushed over to the counter and grabbed the case. Tracey was beside him in a second. Ever so gently she stopped him putting the case under the counter. She opened the unfastened lid and gasped.

'Mr Blair! This is no way for a grown man to approach financial matters.'

Jossy hung his head like a schoolboy being given a dressing down by teacher. Tracey pulled out a bill.

'Carpenter. For new shelves. Dated two months ago.' Tracey's glance demanded an answer.

'He'll wait. I said I'd try to get him Cup Final tickets – next year.'

Tracey dipped again. 'Rates, first quarter . . .'

Jossy broke in confidently. 'I've promised to start paying on the never-never. I hear they never hassle businessmen.'

Tracey was not impressed. She pulled a bill printed in red out of the case. Her eyes nearly popped out as she read it. 'Final demand. Electricity. One hundred and fifty-six pounds – or else!'

Jossy had no answer. He mimed having his throat cut. Tracey began methodically taking the bills out and organising them into 'urgent' and 'not so urgent' piles. Jossy watched approvingly. Maybe now, he thought, he had a chance of getting things organised.

THREE

Jossy Blair's fortunes were about to take a turn for the better – or at least he hoped they were. With that in mind he was standing outside Nelson's betting shop with its windows full of various types of sporting scenes, weighing up the form. He thought about putting a few quid on a horse called Ocean Fury but decided against since he never went on cruises. He gave the thumbs down to Artist's Azure because he did not know any painters. His face lit up, however, when he spotted a horse called McDonald's Bullet in the three o'clock at Uttoxeter.

Jossy's betting worked on instinct. He had played his one and only first team match at St James' Park, Newcastle, alongside Malcolm McDonald. That was enough. His eyes twinkled and he began to whistle as he counted his money. Ricky Sweet, his dour face set as usual, was passing by and he noticed how cheerful Jossy was.

'Won the pools, Mr Blair?'

Jossy recognised him and could not resist a dig. 'Oh, it's a Grasshopper. Do you rub your legs together in the long grass and make a buzzing noise?'

'Funny one,' replied Ricky through his teeth.

Jossy was eager to place his bet. 'Out of my way sonny. I'm just off to take Mr Nelson to the cleaners. I've picked myself a winner.'

Ricky's eyebrows shot up with surprise. He stroked his chin with his finger. 'What system do you use? Timeform, owt like that?'

Jossy curled up his nose in disgust. 'System? Don't talk to me about systems. I don't believe in all that jargon – according to hypotenuse this, and twice the square root of that. Us Geordies work on instinct. Be it football or fillies – the racing kind of course – you've got to feel it right here!' He pressed his right fist to his heart in a way that Sir Laurence Olivier would have dug.

Ricky sensed that he was in the presence of a chancer. 'You'll feel it in your pocket if you don't have a system.'

Jossy paused, tapping the racing paper with his hand. 'What do you know about horse racing anyway?'

Ricky spoke confidently. 'I know all about horses. My dad used to be a National Hunt jockey and he's always going on about courses, conditions, owner's ambitions, that sort of thing.'

'I don't suppose your dad said anything about the three o'clock at Uttoxeter?' There was a pleading look in Jossy's eyes.

'Well, my dad doesn't really give tips. We play a game together. He picks horses by experience but I put the variables he tells me about through my computer.'

The look of surprise on Jossy's face showed that he probably thought variables were a side order at a Chinese take-away.

'Geddaway with you! You're having me on.'

'No. Give me the paper.'

Ricky took the paper and turned to the Uttoxeter card. He closed his eyes and for a second stood like a medium in mid-trance. Then he started murmuring to himself. 'High wind. Going should be firm.' He opened his eyes. 'I'd like to double check this on my computer but it has to be Hall of Fame. Look, it's 10 to 1.'

Jossy didn't bother to look. 'I've been up and down

that card all day. Hall of Fame hasn't got an earthly!
My instinct . . .'

'Which never lets you down?' chipped in Ricky.

Jossy gave him an old-fashioned look. 'You're either
pulling my leg or you've got your variables in a twist,
sunshine. I say McDonald's Bullet.'

'And I say you might as well stick your money down
the drain.'

Ricky marched off. Jossy went into Nelson's shop to
put his money where his instinct was.

A couple of hours later Jossy was stewing over the result
of the three o'clock at Uttoxeter. How could that kid
have picked the winner? Hall of Fame had won easily.
But surely all that stuff about his dad and his computer
had been pure flannel!

The bell clanged as a group of kids came into the
shop. Jossy stopped counting the small change in his till
and looked up – at a trio of Grasshoppers led by Ricky
Sweet. 'You haven't come to scoff at my system I hope.'
Jossy tried to be calm.

Ricky did not seem to be in a scoffing mood. 'I told
you, my system works. You should have listened.'

Ross Nelson stepped forward and Jossy noticed that
he was carrying a thick brown envelope. 'What's in
there? The last will and testament of the Glipton
Grasshoppers?'

Ross ignored this. He looked at Jossy the way J.R.
would look at a rival oil baron in 'Dallas'. Jossy sensed
that a moment of fate had arrived. Tracey Gaunt came
into the shop and stopped when she sussed the drama.

Ross was fiddling with the tucked-in flap of the
envelope. Eyes widened all round as he slid out the
contents – a wad of crisp, brown, ten-pound notes. His
voice was quiet: 'My dad says that if success is worth
having then it's worth paying for, Mr Blair.' Jossy

looked subdued. 'If you will agree to be our manager, you can take this three hundred pounds here and now. My dad regards it as an investment. We need a new image for our club so we need a new set of shirts in say . . .'

'Red and white.' Harvey McGuinn rarely stayed low profile for long. 'We'll model ourselves on Manchester United. They're the best.'

A dig from Ricky shut him up.

Ross continued: 'We'll play in any colours you choose, Mr Blair. By my reckoning new gear will cost £150. The other £150 you can keep as an emergency kitty – to be used for the Grasshoppers as and when necessary.'

Jossy looked across the shop to Tracey and received a knowing wink. There were certainly wheels turning within wheels. And what was that about the choices open to beggars? He began to make up his mind.

'What do you say, Mr Blair?'

'Jossy, son.' The words brought faint smiles to Ross and the rest. 'I say – why don't we play in the famous black and white stripes of the Mighty Magpies?' The boys nodded vigorously. 'I say – change the name of the club to something strong and powerful like . . . the Glipton Giants.' There were more nods of agreement. A lump came into Jossy's throat as he uttered the last words. 'And we'll call our ground . . . St James' Park.'

'Yes!' The voices of Ross, Ricky, Harvey and Tracey were as one. Tracey came round to where Jossy was standing by the till. She shuffled the notes back into the envelope and opened the old suitcase full of bills. 'Electricity £156' glowed bright red from the bill at the top of the pile. Again Tracey slipped Jossy a knowing wink.

There was more for Jossy's plate. Ricky stepped forward quickly and his usually dour face softened a bit as he spoke. 'I will offer you a weekly tip on the horses,

31

worked out by my unique system.'

Jossy felt as if all his birthdays had come on the same day. There was a gleam in his eyes as he addressed them. 'You know, you little lads – and lass – have just put a spark of light back in my life.' He looked round and saw that he was getting no more than seven out of ten for sincerity. So he turned practical. 'But hang on, what about the manager that you've already got?'

Harvey was quick to reply. 'Oh, Albert will be no trouble. He'll be happy that you're taking over. Albert's not nasty and big-headed enough to be a successful manager.'

'Hey, just you watch it!' snapped Jossy, but half joking, 'Brian Clough's not the only one who slaps cocky players down when required.'

The three boys turned and left the shop. Jossy turned to Tracey. 'Now you wouldn't be the Fairy Godmother that got me all this today?'

Tracey grinned. 'Well, I did make a few suggestions to Mr Nelson that I reckon set the ball rolling.'

Jossy was musing. 'So if I pay the electric bill and that Ricky comes up with the goods . . .'

'. . . and the Giants flock here for boots and the rest of the gear,' Tracey chipped in.

'That's my girl,' said Josey.

Tracey had produced a small parcel from her pocket and was toying with it nervously. She handed it to Jossy. He looked surprised and a shade embarrassed. His expression did not change once he got the paper off to disclose a small atomiser bottle of cologne.

'Fleurs de Rose pour Gentilhommes,' in Jossy's sing-song Geordie voice it sounded like a mincer at work. 'What is it, pet?'

Tracey took the bottle from him and in a flash squirted a little on to Jossy's cheek. He jumped back as if attacked by jellyfish. Tracey giggled. 'It's cologne.

You put it on after a bath or a shave. It smells nice.'

Jossy shook his head firmly. 'Scent, lassie? Me! Wearing scent! I'm sorry love, but where I come from the fellas' don't use cosmetics. You'd never live it down. It could brand a whole family – for generations.'

Tracey laughed even louder.

The scene inside the gym of the Glipton Community Centre was like a parade ground in ancient Rome as the legions awaited an inspection by Julius Ceasar. Over a dozen Giants in extra-clean training gear booted balls around. There was much less horse-play than on a normal training night. Albert had been a bit worried that Jossy might want him to leave the club but Ross had reassured him. 'He needs a solid right-arm like you, Albert. Jossy Blair is a genius on football tactics and a great motivator. But he couldn't organise a cold shower in a cloudburst.' Ross had not, of course, voiced this opinion in front of Jossy.

Albert decided to make a good impression on the new boss by getting the squad into action. He gathered them all around.

'OK, you lot. All lie flat on the floor on your bellies. I'll whistle twenty times and I want a press-up each time.'

The boys all got into position. Albert went the whole hog. He got into press-up position too. With great difficulty he got his whistle to his mouth and left it there. He blew the whistle. Bottoms shot up; bony arms bent; gasps wheezed everywhere. Albert was not to know the shambles all around him. Eyes tight shut, he pressed, wheezed and whistled half a dozen times. The sight nearly made Jossy laugh out loud as he slipped into the gym.

At the sight of their new supremo some of the lads tried harder, but the overall effect was ludicrous. Jossy tip-toed over to the sagging form of Albert. Ever so gently he placed his right foot in the middle of Albert's back. It was the last straw. The whistle shot out of Albert's mouth and he collapsed flat.

'Observe, Giants. I have just illustrated an important point of football. An extra ounce of effort produces an extra pound of performance – sometimes.'

'Doesn't the Geordie know we've gone metric!' said Harvey loudly.

Jossy was laughing as he helped Albert up. 'Come on, old son. You didn't mind my little joke, did you?'

Albert grinned a pale grin. Jossy's mood changed. He became brisk, almost business-like. The next remark was aimed at all of them. 'Next time I come in here I want to see Giants. I want to see footballers at their work, not a living picture of a hospital for wounded seals. Why were we doing press-ups?'

'To get fit,' Albert offered.

Jossy began again, apparently addressing one of the neon strip lights in the roof. 'Extra muscle in the arms and shoulders is useless to a footballer. It's in the legs we want strength.' His gaze panned down to the boys. 'Where?'

'In the legs,' came back the cry.

'Tell me again.'

'In the legs,' the volume was the same. One or two added, 'Jossy.'

'Before we go any further lads,' Jossy's voice was crisp with authority, 'a point of order. In future, on match days and at training, nobody in this club will address me as anything else other than BOSS! OK?'

'OK,' murmured the boys.

'OK – what?'

'OK BOSS!'

'Obergruppen führer,' was Harvey's contribution. It did not go unnoticed by the new boss.

'Right, Giants,' Jossy's voice held a parade-ground tone, 'form a single line. Quick!'

The boys scrambled into some semblance of a straight line. Jossy, hands clasped behind his back, began to inspect them, with Albert bringing up the rear at a respectful distance. When he drew level with Harvey, Jossy scowled.

'In future, no vests, bodywarmers or the like will be worn underneath the club playing strip.' His eyes burned like a laser at Harvey. 'Players are allowed, however, to wear, er – *devices* approved by the manager.' As the boys exchanged puzzled looks, Jossy turned to Albert. 'Make a note, Albert. We'll need twelve Glipton Corporation dustbin liners for the match on Saturday.'

Albert was none the wiser but nodded anyway. Jossy moved level with Glenn who was toying with a few strands of his light blue hair. Selly stood next in line. 'I want all mirrors covered in all dressing-rooms, home and away.' He looked at Selly's Mohican top-knot. 'Report for extra heading practice at two o'clock on Saturday.'

A few of the others giggled. Jossy was now facing Ricky. Gone was the strict disciplinarian look. Jossy leaned forward and half-whispered: 'I don't have to lecture you do I, Ricky old son? Just keep in mind that it's Newton Abbot this weekend. I'd like something at about 8 to 1. But it's up to you, of course.'

At the end of the line Jossy stopped. He took a couple of paces back and gave his last message. 'I want all of you and as many parents, friends, fans, etcetera, as possible at St James' Park – formerly Canalside Stadium – at nine o'clock prompt on Saturday.'

'But we don't kick off until one,' squeaked Harvey.

Jossy walked back to the line and leaned until he was nose to nose with Harvey. 'All the more time to work on our new image then, isn't it?' His eyes swept over all the

Giants. 'Bring old gear. We've got some mucky work to do.'

The transformation of Canalside Stadium was almost complete by noon on Saturday. Swathes of black and white, two feet wide, now decorated the tatty grandstand. The rusty rail that went round the pitch shone with fresh paint. Bob Nelson, sporting a black-and-white scarf, came down from the step-ladder to admire the way he had put up one of the goal nets. He rubbed at his right eye which was quickly puffing up into a real shiner from frequent attacks by the thick rubber bands that held the nets to the posts. After a lightning inspection Jossy Blair called them all to the end of the grandstand where a black-and-white flag was draped over a new sign on the wall.

'Gather around folks, I'd like to say a few words in honour of today.' A couple of the boys exchanged winks and comic groans. Jossy looked very solemn. 'As some of you might know, my own football career was cut short in its prime. But today is a day of pride for me and I hope all of you. So I'd like to ask Mr Bob Nelson, our club's main benefactor, to step up here and do the honours.'

The players and friends applauded as Bob stepped forward. He was not the kind of bloke to miss out on an opportunity to say a few words. 'Giants, fellow parents and friends . . .'

Five minutes later Bob was still rabbiting on, but a savage look from Ross brought him to the point. 'So I'd like to unveil this commemorative plaque to mark a new dawn in the history of football in Glipton.'

There was a trickle of applause as Bob pulled a string and the Giants' flag fell to reveal the sign *St James' Park. Home of Glipton Giants F.C.*

Ten minutes before kick-off the Giants were raring to go. The boys danced about nervously in their shorts, socks and boots, waiting for the hallowed black-and-white shirts to be issued. But Jossy had a couple of extra rituals up his sleeve. He picked up a bundle of dustbin liners marked 'Glipton District Council', and selected one for the demonstration. The boys noticed that arm-holes had been cut in the side and a slit in the top. Jossy beckoned to Ricky to join him. 'Come over here, my son, and be the first to try my thermal consolation.'

'What?' asked Selly.

'I think he means insulation,' whispered Harvey.

The rest of the lads gawped as Jossy dressed Ricky in the bin liner, carefully tightening the mid-section with Sellotape. Then he pushed Ricky off on a parade around the room like a Paris fashion model.

Some of the lads giggled but it did not stop Jossy. 'Observe how loose the equipment is. No bulk. The body can sweat freely. The elements cannot penetrate.' He paused for breath. 'Right, Giants, put on liners!'

They scrambled into the liners and began taping each other up. By the time they had finished, Jossy had laid an ancient Subbuteo table football board out on the floor and was carefully placing red and blue plastic 'men' in formation. The boys noticed that there were only ten of the red players.

'Why are the reds a man short, Boss?' asked Harvey.

Jossy gave him the eagle glare, then pulled a clenched fist from his pocket. He opened his palm to disclose a painted Santa Claus of the kind used to decorate Christmas cakes. 'I lost a counter, so I decided this would represent you, Harvey.'

Harvey as usual had an answer. 'I'm going to need half a dozen reindeer to patrol my line, Boss.'

The boys were far too excited to take Jossy's talk of 'dominating the mid-field' and 'keeping tight at the back' very seriously. Soon each had slipped on a new shirt and then filed out past Jossy and Albert. Both men were nearly in tears as they patted each back in turn.

Ross was the last out. He looked at Jossy and whispered, 'We'll do our best, Boss.'

'I know son. By, it takes me back. I used to run out last.'

'I know – Boss.'

With ten minutes to go the Farley Hawks were making the match a real baptism of fire for the Giants. A flukey lob had flown over Harvey's head to make it 1-0. Now only sterling work by Ricky Sweet at the heart of the defence was keeping them at bay. Jossy, however, had a plan. He whispered something in Tracey's ear and she set off towards the Hawks' goal. It was manned by a tall, blond kid with an earring. Tracey leaned casually against the post, caught the goalie's attention and gave him the big come-on look. 'What's your name handsome?'

'Kevin,' said the goalie.

Tracey looked upfield casually and saw that Glenn and Selly were building up an attack. Before the goalie could look back at the action, she made her move.

'I'm into toga parties. Like to come to one tonight?'

The timing was perfect. Kevin was looking in the wrong direction as Ross flicked a long ball from Selly inside the far post. Kevin's popularity with the other Hawks took a rapid nose dive. The Giants were jubilant.

Five minutes later Tracey struck again. Seeing Ricky charging over the half-way line, she flopped against the post in what looked like a fainting fit. Kevin swooped to her aid. Ricky's shot flew into the open goal. A couple of Giants crowded round Tracey, who kept up the act. 'Get the trainer please. I'm in desperate need of the magic sponge.'

At the final whistle the Giants mobbed Jossy and the Hawks told goalie Kevin what they thought of him.

There was only one final ritual left on the great day and it was of prime importance to Jossy. He stood outside Nelson's betting shop, not even bothering to check on the runners and riders in the paper. Ricky came round the corner and joined him, a computer print-out in his hand.

'Here's your tip, Boss.' Ricky winked at Jossy and then began to read off the piece of paper: 'Variables. Heavy going, but that's usual at Newton Abbot. Slight wind. Dad's advice – horse has just got over tummy trouble. So – the winner will be Merry Marauder.'

Jossy looked at him as if he was Aladdin's genie. He counted out three pounds and walked like a man in a trance into the bookie's.

Ten minutes later the voice on the tannoy in the shop echoed into the street. 'Three furlongs to go at Newton Abbot. Merry Marauder in the lead by three lengths.' Jossy began a jig of delight. 'But up on the rails comes Highland Prince.' Jossy froze. 'And Merry Marauder seems to be breathing heavily. It might be the strong gusty wind.'

Jossy glowered at Ricky. 'You said *slight* wind.'

Ricky shrugged.

The tannoy crackled out again. 'So at the line it's Highland Prince by four lengths. Highland Prince the winner.'

Jossy tore up the slip and lobbed the bits to the wind. He pretended to be mad. Running after Ricky, fists raised, he shouted, 'I'll teach you to get your variables in a twist, kidda!'

FOUR

Ross Nelson was reliving the glories of the Giants' great day. His mind went over the fun of the various dressing-room rituals, particularly the bin liner episode. He action-replayed his own goal several times and he burst out with loud laughter recalling Tracey's sex-bomb attack on the Hawk's goalie.

He jumped out of bed, slipped on his new Giants' tracksuit – another money-spinning line for Jossy's shop – and jogged along the landing to the bathroom. His dad was greeted with song as he passed the bathroom door: 'We are black, we are white, we are really dynamite, and the Giants' go marching along.'

It crossed Bob's mind that he had never heard his son so happy. He shouted to Ross. 'Don't go mad in there.' His next remark was more serious. 'I expect all the talent scouts from the other clubs will be flocking to see you soon. The Giants aren't bad, but we'll have to think of you playing in better company.'

'Don't be daft, Dad. I'm happy where I am.' Ross's voice was troubled.

'I'm off now. But think about it. We can't let the grass grow under our feet.'

As he listened to his dad's footsteps go off down the stairs, Ross thought to himself: '. . . and the grass is always greener on the other side of the hill.' Then he went back to brushing his almost perfect teeth.

Jossy's voice rang out clear over St James' Park: 'Stop

throwing it to Ricky. 'Here, Rick, set it up. I'll show you how to do it.'

Again the ball was airborne and Ross leapt like the others. This time a thwack echoed round the ground and Harvey felt something fly past his ear and thump into the net. Ross danced away like a drunken Apache, leaping and prancing. The other Giants gawped. Jossy said quietly, 'Fluke.' But he was not sure.

All this was being watched by a mysterious figure in the bushes at the side of St James' Park. He was a middle-aged man in a black tracksuit with a balaclava helmet hiding his face. The man lowered his binoculars and scribbled a few words in a notebook. Then he resumed his scrutiny of the Giants. who were now getting down to some serious practice.

Ross Nelson was really revelling in his success with the overhead kick. He would not settle down to practise with the others. Jossy boned him as he went off on a dribble.

'Here, Zico,' said Jossy curtly, 'I'd like you over here a minute – if it's no trouble.'

Ross trotted over.

'In America they have awards for what they call Most Valuable Player. I think we should have one this season.'

'I'd be lucky to get a quid if I put the lot of you on the market,' replied Jossy. He turned to the rest of the team. 'Gather round, you lot! I will now announce the squad for this weekend's Crompton Cup 5-a-side finals.' The boys gathered round quietly. Jossy began reading. 'The line-up will be: Goal – Harvey. At the back – Ricky. Up front – Glenn, Selly and Wayne.' There was a shocked gasp from the boys. 'Substitute – Ross.'

Jossy began to explain his surprise selection. 'I want fast passing, sharp shooting, no dribbling.' Harvey shook his head slowly. Ross said nothing. He just began to walk, head down, towards his father's car. After a few yards he began to run.

'You shouldn't have dropped him,' muttered Harvey.

Jossy glowered at them all. 'I'm the manager here. I do what's best for the team.'

Bob Nelson was half-asleep in the driving seat of his Mercedes when Ross arrived at the car. There was something wrong, Bob was sure. The head was down and the smile missing. Ross scrambled into the back seat.

'What's got into you?'

'Nowt. Let's just go home.' There was a crack in the voice that disturbed Bob.

'You're not injured, are you son?'

Ross spoke sharply. 'Let's just get away from here. I don't want to see this stupid football ground again. Or that Geordie idiot.'

'What's happened?' asked Bob.

'He's made me sub for the rotten 5-a-side!'

The news hit Bob like a missile. He simply did not believe it. 'Impossible! You're their best player!'

As both Nelsons sat tight-lipped in the car, the mystery figure who had been watching the game appeared and tapped at the window. Bob started violently, thinking that the balaclava-clad figure was a mugger. The man removed his headgear to reveal iron-grey hair and a neatly clipped moustache. His eyes were keen, if a little fanatical. Bob wound down the window and the newcomer introduced himself.

'Mr Nelson? I'm Dave Sharkey and I'd like to have a word with you if I may.'

Bob's first reaction was to get rid of the fellow, but the notebook the man was clutching made him hesitate. Also the name had rung a bell.

'Dave who?' asked Bob.

'Dave Sharkey.' The man glowed with what he

44

obviously considered was a bit of proper pride. 'I'm the manager of Ecclestone Express F.C. You might have heard of us.'

A bit of the tension was gone from Bob's voice. 'You're not the bloke who makes the team turn out on *parade*. Kit inspections and all that?'

Sharkey was not at all amused by the slightly mocking tone. 'Proper kit. Clean boots. No detail is too small if you're success-minded.' Bob paid attention. 'I have had spies watching your son in recent games and they've given me good reports.' Ross's mood had now also changed for the better. 'I think your son, Mr Nelson, is wasting his time with the – er – Giants.' Sharkey said it as though he had a bad smell near his nose. 'And I'd like him for my team.'

Ross and Bob were both pleasantly gob-smacked. Sharkey saw this and reached inside the small rucksack on his back and pulled out his ace card. He held up an Express shirt, an explosion of violent red with gold trim and a gold lightning flash across the chest. Ross's eyes stuck out like organ stops. Bob, typically, felt the material.

'Good gear that.' Bob's voice was full of enthusiasm. 'Your lot are in the Crompton Cup 5-a-side finals aren't you?'

Sharkey bristled with confidence like a true fanatic. 'I would say, without boasting, that my team are in fact the favourites for the competition.' He aimed a sneer in the general direction of St James' Park. 'My squad's training is based on the sound principles of possession football and work rate.' Bob and Ross goggled at him as though he was Paul Daniels sawing a lady in half. 'We do not fool around with flashy overhead kicks and random sharp shooting.' Sharkey's eyes were now blazing. 'Express are fit, finely-tuned and dedicated. We integrate like a Panzer division.'

Something in this fervour worried Bob but it was no time to quibble. Fate had dealt the Nelsons a superb hand. 'Spot on, Squire,' said Bob.

'Can I play centre-forward?' Ross had the air of Oliver Twist in the gruel queue.

Sharkey looked solemn 'Never forget that I am manager, son. But you will be the striker in the 5-a-side. I want total commitment and a hundred and ten per cent effort.

The two men walked away in deep discussion. Ross muttered to himself: 'I'll show you Jossy Blair – you and your Pigmies!'

Within a few days, the word of Ross's desertion had got round most of the Giants. Jossy Blair, however, had other worries. Trade was still very slack and the pile of bills he was staring at got no smaller. He spotted Tracey Gaunt coming over the street to join him and he tried to hide the case full of bills. Tracey was up to his tricks. 'It's no good trying to hide from reality, Jossy. Those bills won't pay themselves.'

Jossy looked guilty. He changed the subject. 'Do you reckon Ross really means to join the Express?'

'Means to!' Tracey looked at Jossy as though he was mad. 'He's training with them now and flogging the pavements at night. He's determined to be their star man.'

'I reckon he'll be back in the fold before the season's out.' Jossy did not sound too sure. He moved on quickly to other business. 'When are you going to send in the £25 entry fee for the 5-a-side?'

'I've been extra busy with my homework.' Tracey was a real hard worker. 'We have to have the money in by Thursday, so I'll pop round to the secretary's house tomorrow and pay up.'

Tracey had been fiddling in her pocket ever since she

46

came into the shop. Now she took out a small gift-wrapped parcel and handed it to Jossy. 'This is a small memento of our first win. I hope you'll accept it.'

Josy took it as though it was a red hot coal. With very little ceremony he took the paper off to reveal a chain with a medallion on it in the form of a magpie sporting a top hat. Jossy twiddled it round, a look of puzzlement on his face.

'It's very nice, love, Dead cute. But . . .'

'But what?' Tracey was annoyed.

Jossy wriggled. 'Well, I know all the macho lads down the discos and on the telly adverts wear these things. That's to stop people noticing that they've got no hairs on their chests!' He waited for a laugh that did not come. 'But us Geordies – we just don't wear jewellery.'

'It's not jewellery.' The words filtered out between gritted teeth.

Jossy got the message. He fastened the chain around his neck. 'I'll wear it just for you, pet. If I pull the front of my vest right up, nobody'll be any the wiser.'

This time he got a smile.

The shop doorbell rang and Albert Hanson came in, panting heavily. He was carrying an enormous hold-all full of unwashed football kit. Bits of black-and-white material stuck out of the unzipped top.

'Somebody else will have to wash the kit this week, Jossy. Our washing machine's just gone on the blink.'

'Don't worry, old son,' said Jossy, 'We only need six sets this week. Leave them on the counter. I'll persuade somebody to wash them. Right now tactics for Saturday are top of our list. Get the blackboard out for me.'

While Albert got the board out, Jossy paced the floor waiting for his stars. Glenn and Selly were the first to arrive and their punk image was now just about over the top. Their collection of pins and chains made them look like a pair of monkey puzzles. Jossy was in like a bullet. 'If I had that much old iron, I'd start a scrap-yard.'

Glenn was quick to respond. He pointed at Jossy's new medallion. 'Aren't you a bit long in the tooth to be a poser, Boss?'

Before Jossy could attempt a reply, Ricky came in. He had taken to wearing his Giants strip as a pullover and today it was not looking its cleanest.

'You've still got Saturday's muck all over that strip. Put it in the bag.' Jossy prodded Ricky in the chest.

'But it's lucky to keep it on,' Ricky was a very stubborn lad at times.

'Lucky maybe, but not very hygienic,' chipped in Tracey.

'Off!' roared Jossy. Ricky shook his head and jutted out his chin. By now there were half a dozen Giants in the shop. Jossy turned to them with a wicked grin.

'Strip retrieval detail . . .' The boys grinned. Jossy continued in military vein: 'Are you ready?'

'Aye, aye, sir.'

'Charge!' Jossy led the sortie. They pounced on Ricky and after a struggle got the shirt off him. Jossy was holding it aloft when the doorbell rang. Everybody turned. It was the Nelsons. Bob led the way with a solemn look. He had a parcel in his hands. Ross was close behind wearing a flashy, new Express tracksuit. As usual Harvey missed the mood of the moment.

'Oh, Rossy's jumped aboard the Express now. So he's dressing up like Jimmy Savile.'

Nobody so much as smiled. Jossy gave Harvey a hard glance. Bob walked over to Jossy with a very stiff expression on his face. He spoke like a judge dishing out a death sentence. 'Here is my lad's gear. Strip, shorts, socks. He is no longer a member of this club.'

Jossy would not lift his hands to accept the parcel. He equalled Bob's stony look. 'Now hang on a tick, Bob. Just because I made Ross sub . . .'

'That's not the point.' Bob's tone now became insulting. 'We are moving to a club where they run things professionally. I want the best for my lad. Your operation is a bit too sloppy for my liking, Blair.'

Jossy was shaking with emotion. His pale face was flushed. 'It wasn't sloppy when we were sticking goals past the Hawks, Nelson!'

Bob paced to the counter and put down the parcel. Ricky and Harvey exchanged hostile looks with Ross. Tracey began scribbling near the till. As he was about to open the door, Bob turned. 'There's also the small matter of £150 of my money in your bank account. I'll expect a cheque for the full amount soon.'

As Jossy's face turned white, Tracey advanced like a budding Boadicea. She waved a cheque and a pen under Jossy's nose.

'Sign,' she said firmly.

Jossy raised no objection. He signed the cheque. Tracey handed it to Bob with a flourish.

'I thought you might mention that, *Mr* Nelson. As Acting Secretary of the Glipton Giants, I wouldn't want you to think our administration was as *sloppy* as our play. So please take this. Our account with you is settled – in full.'

Bob stuffed the cheque casually into his pocket. He opened the door and left. Ross followed.

'Judas!' hissed Harvey.

'At least I can *pay* for a seat at The Last Supper.' Ross's wit had not been affected by all the aggro.

Jossy broke the silence. He turned to Tracey and said softly, 'I like your style, pet. But you realise that now we're well and truly skint?'

'You wouldn't have us keep blood money, would you?'

The answer impressed Jossy. But it did not solve their immediate problem. 'What are we going to do about the twenty-five quid for the Crompton 5-a-side competition?'

'We're going to show some initiative. We've got about thirty-six hours to raise the cash. I suggest we put our skates on!'

FIVE

The quest for cash took Jossy to the steps of the betting shop. Ricky had followed him there and was pleading for another chance.

'Oh, come on, Jossy, you've got to trust me. They'll be off at Newcastle in ten minutes. Sylvia's Sweetheart is 8 to 1 . . .'

'So was Merry Marauder. And it sank without trace.' Jossy stuck his head back in the racing pages and Ricky continued his appeal.

'Look. Now and again I admit my system malfunctions. But even my Dad says this horse is a good 'un. It's a very strong horse. There's a strong headwind forecast. It can't lose. Please put your money on Sylvia's Sweetheart.'

A silly romantic look came over Jossy's face. There was a touch of Robbie Burns in his voice. 'Sylvia's Sweetheart. By lad, that takes me back. I used to be just that. Her name was Sylvia McSparron; she had white blonde hair. What a cracker! She used to pay for herself at the pictures. Ahead of her time you see!'

'So, your instinct and my system fall in line.' Ricky reeled in hard. 'Put a pound on and we win eight. Put two on – and Crampton Cup here we come.'

Ten minutes later Ricky and Jossy were on tenterhooks as Sylvia's Sweetheart led the field into the straight. The crackly voice on the tannoy built up the excitement. 'With two furlongs left, Sylvia's Sweetheart up by two lengths on Shortofabob. Wind is really gusting into their faces now as Shortofabob makes his effort. And Sylvia's Sweetheart is tiring. Shortofabob sweeps through and wins.'

Ricky's face was a picture. He hung his head. Jossy raised the paper as if to clout Ricky. 'Strong horse. Great against the wind! Two quid down the Swanee.'

The money-spinning schemes of the other Giants were by and large more imaginative.

The garden of Selly's house now resembled a scene from 'The Wizard of Oz'. Selly and Glenn, in full punk gear, were in the process of transforming the hair style of an eight-year-old. The boy was sitting on a chair beside a sign reading *Exclusive Punk Hair Styles*, 35p. Glenn was turning one side of the kid's head spiky with a comb and lacquer, while Selly sprayed the other half green. Their victim looked as though he was having second thoughts about his new image.

'Vandals! What are you doing to my Jason?' A big lady carrying a bag from the local supermarket swooped in like a vulture and grabbed her offspring. The lady kicked over the sign and Jason got a sound smack on the ear for wasting his pocket money.

Ricky had not let the setback with the horses get him down. He and Harvey had thought up a really bright idea; car washing. They had set up shop in a busy side street in the centre of Glipton. A shopper had given them their first job – the works for 75 pence – and they were hard at it with water and wash leathers.

Both boys looked up the street and saw a familiar car slowly approaching – Bob Nelson's white Mercedes. Behind the car jogged a very weary Ross. His father was shouting encouragement to him through the car window. It was just too good a chance to miss.

Harvey and Ricky ducked down behind the car they were washing. They waited until Ross was level with them and let fly with a bucket of water each. It drenched him. Ross stopped in his tracks. 'I'll get you for this. Wait until Saturday.'

Harvey and Ricky sprinted off for all they were worth, but Ross was too bushed to chase.

'Come on. No slacking.' Bob's voice echoed down the street. He had not even seen the ducking.

Inside the Glipton Community Centre Albert Hanson was witnessing a brave, if dangerous, attempt by Jossy to raise cash. The advert had read, 'Wanted – active model to work with Karate class.' Now Jossy stood in a floppy judo jacket and trousers waiting for a very small, but very powerful, Japanese gentleman to let rip. Six students watched attentively. Already Jossy had a bruise coming up on his cheek.

The instructor laid hold of Jossy yet again. He addressed the class. 'Now observe treatment of street mugger.'

Jossy, eyebrows raised, played to the gallery. 'Who, me?'

Next second he was flying over the room. He landed with a crunch that made Albert wince. It was clear to Albert that this was going to be the toughest fiver that Jossy would ever earn.

One of the most famous landmarks in Glipton High Street is Tuttle's Pork Shop. It has blue and white tiles on the outside and inside is a riot of delicious smells from the traditional delicacies: pies, puddings, pastes of every variety. Despite the advent of the supermarket, Simeon Tuttle always did a roaring trade. Just before half-past five on the day of the great Giants' fund-raising campaign, he smiled happily as his new shop assistant did her thing yet again. All right, Tracey Gaunt was his niece, but one day she would make a fortune in business if she put her mind to it.

Tracey persuaded a lady who already had bought chops and a joint to take six ounces of pease pudding 'as a little treat for the man of the house'.

Mr Tuttle pulled down the blind and changed the sign to 'Closed'. He turned to Tracey. 'You're a natural sales girl, lass. Now about that scheme you outlined earlier . . .'

'OK, Uncle Simeon. Take my word for it. If you speculate the way I suggest, you're bound to accumulate.'

They went into a huddle.

A couple of hours later the Giants assembled in Jossy's shop for the great reckon-up. A few sniggers were aimed at Jossy's cuts and bruises from the Karate class, but his solemn face brought a silence to proceedings.

'Right, lads. I can see by your faces that it's not gone very well. But let's put the takings on the counter.'

One by one the fund-raisers stepped forward.

Glenn and Selly looked apologetic. Selly tried to put up a bit of a show. 'Hair-dressing is a very competitive game, Jossy.'

'How much?' Jossy's words tore through the flannel.

'Seventy pence,' Selly spoke very quietly.

Glenn put his spoke in. 'We had just over a quid at one stage. But one of the mums demanded the 35 pence back to buy shampoo to get the purple out!'

'Purple,' murmured Jossy. He picked up the money and Albert rang it up on the till. The rest of them mooched up with various tales of failure. By the time it was Jossy's turn to show his hand, they had £3.30 in the kitty for the Crompton Cup.

Jossy looked woefully at Albert and placed £2.50 on the counter. 'Sorry lads. I'm afraid I could only take being a karate chopping block for half an hour.'

The gag fell on stony ground. They had raised precisely £5.80. One or two of the boys started towards the door. The bell clanged and in breezed Tracey looking as though she had won the pools. She stared at them as though they were creatures from another planet. 'If the Express players walked in here now they'd think you lot had given up. You look like Napoleon's army on the retreat from Moscow.'

Jossy leapt in. 'That's enough of that, lassie. This is no time for jokes.'

Harvey continued the counter-attack. 'Some right you've got to come in here shouting your mouth off. We've been sweating cobs trying to raise money and you've been swanning about.'

Tracey moved to the counter and looked at the total of their efforts registered on the till. '£5.80. Pathetic!'

Even Albert was now incensed by her attitude. 'Easy, love,' he cast an eye to Jossy's wounds, 'some people *suffered* raising that cash.'

Tracey's buoyant, almost aggressive mood baffled them. She realised it was time to play her ace. 'It just so happens that we women do have our strong points – though I know some of you men doubt it.' She paused for maximum effect. 'I must admit that I have not actually *suffered* in the Giants' cause but . . .' she pulled five fivers out from her pocket . . . 'by a combination of brains and application, I have managed to raise the entrance money for the Crompton Cup.'

'I don't believe it.' Jossy's eyes glowed with a mixture of affection and admiration. 'You got the money, all above board?'

'Oh yes,' said Tracey. 'But hadn't you better get working double quick on tactics for Saturday?'

The roar of the crowd percolated through to the Express dressing-room as Dave Sharkey prepared his men to take on the Giants in the 5-a-side Final. Each side had battled through the preliminary rounds and now it was the crunch. Bob Nelson stood proudly at Sharkey's right hand. He was wearing a greasy grin, a brand new tracksuit and a baseball cap in Express colours. Bob had been made 'Honorary Assistant Manager' for the occasion.

The boys sat heads down with worry and concentration except for Ross who was on edge. He bounced a ball repeatedly and danced up and down. Dave Sharkey, wearing a suit and tie, had to have words with him.

'Nelson. Sit down and pay attention. This is a very important match.'

Ross did as he was told but he did not seem to be listening very much as Sharkey went into his act.

'I want all of you to go into this match full of confidence. Our opponents – the, er, Giants – are a slapdash outfit. They have little method or discipline.' He paused and ran his eagle eye over his men. 'I want all of you to look out for diagonal runs from Nelson. Provide him with first time balls. Now. Attention!'

Ross was new to the military type rituals of the Express. He was last to his feet as Sharkey and his father set off on the 'inspection'. In the middle of the line they stopped by a lad called Sawyer. Sharkey knelt down and stared hard at the boy's trainers.

'Sawyer. You know my rules on kit. These laces have mud on them. I'm fining you 50 pence. Collect that later, Serg . . . er – Nelson!'

Bob had to fight to conceal a grin. This bloke was a case. Sharkey stopped at the end of the line.

'I shall now take a seat at the back of the hall. You have been briefed. WIN! Nelson here will be on the touch-line if you need water, sponge, chewing gum.'

Sharkey marched out. The Express lads ran out, Ross hanging back to be last. Bob leaned over to give a last word of encouragement. 'I'll give you two quid for each goal you put past Blair's lot.'

'No,' said Ross with a tough look, 'I'll give *you* two quid.'

In the other dressing-room Jossy was in a subdued mood. There was something more than just edginess about the team. They fidgeted in their gear with their tracksuit tops still on, but they were nowhere near as bouncy as usual. Nerves were not usually a problem with the Giants.

'Keep it up, that's all I'm going to say,' said Jossy, as he prowled, hands thrust deep into the pockets of his tracksuit top. 'This is the big one. Forget about Ross and the rest of the Express. Play your football out there and you'll win.'

Harvey could not bottle up his feelings any longer. 'The crowd are going to fall about when they see us . . .'

'Shut up, Harvey,' Jossy almost snarled. 'We live in a nasty, harsh, commercial age. Forget the crowd. Think of the glory.'

'Wait till Ross Nelson comes near me.' The tension was even getting through to Ricky.

Jossy walked over to the door. 'Get out there and blaze into them.' The lads filed out. Harvey was last.

'Why did she have to . . . ?'

'It's for one game only. We'll be laughing about it tomorrow.'

Harvey left. Jossy looked down at his chest. He pulled the zip of the tracksuit down. A grimace spread over his face but not for long. With a resigned look, he followed the lads out.

The Express lads were lined up like Juventus on an important night in Europe. Ross bobbed up and down

like a jack-in-the-box. His eyes glowed. Ricky led th
Giants out as the tannoy crackled into life. 'Now w
come to the Grand Final of the Crompton Cup com
petition. In the red and gold we have Eccleston
Express, sponsored by Chemical Concrete Ltd.' A wav
of cheering broke out.

There was a strange tone in the rather posh an
nouncer's voice as he began the introduction of th
Giants. 'Their opponents, winners of Group 2, in black
and-white stripes, the Glipton Giants, sponsored by -
The voice spluttered into a muffled laugh that mad
Jossy glare up at a nearby speaker – 'sponsored by, I'r
sorry. . .' The voice regained composure long enough t
say the fateful words: 'Tuttle's Best Tripe.'

Thrusting out his chin, Jossy led the great exposur
He pulled off his tracksuit top to reveal 'Simeon Tuttle'
lettered on the front of his strip and 'Best Tripe' on th
back. The Giants followed his example, revealing th
same slogan. The crowd went into tucks of laughter
The Express team and the Nelsons had hysterics. Th
only genuine smiles, naturally enough, came fror
Tracey Gaunt and Simeon Tuttle, Master Butcher.

The photographer from the *Glipton Bugle* was on ther
like David Attenborough spying a lost tribe of pygmie
He snapped them from every angle, though there wa
not a smile in sight. Harvey at one stage made as thoug
to do a runner but Jossy stopped him. There was no sig
of the charming Geordie smile as he hissed throug
gritted teeth. 'Easy Harvey. We've taken bigger stic
than this. Get out there and let's show them what we'r
made of.'

The referee whistled up the teams for the start of th
game. There were to be two ten-minute halves. Ros
approached the ball to kick off for the Express. H
glared at Ricky. 'We're going to run you lot ragge
Jossy Blair's onions!'

Before Ricky could reply, the referee said to Ross: 'Less of that, son. I've got my eye on you.' Ross gave him the glare treatment too.

The whistle blew. Ross belted the ball to a colleague and raced upfield yelling for it back. Ricky intercepted the pass, paused and was almost felled by Ross's lunging tackle from behind. The referee let it go. Ross passed to the wing. His team-mate out there could not reach the ball. It bounced to Wayne. Ross was furious.

'What's the use of me passing if you're going to mess around?'

There were several angry looks from the other Express players. But they knew what Sharkey's orders were: pass to Nelson. Within seconds the plan paid off. Wayne miskicked for the Giants. Ross pounced on the ball, feinted to run to the wing, turned inside Ricky and slid the ball past Harvey. Ross danced triumphant but the other Express lads did not mob him. There was verbal approval. But Bob was delirious.

'That's my boy. Let's have six. Skin 'em every time.' Bob paced the touch-line like a wolf nearing a chicken farm. Jossy was doing a bit of pacing too. As he passed Bob, he gave him a look, half-matey, half-worried. The sneer he got back was straight from a Hammer horror villain. On the pitch the Express got on the right track again. A fumble by Harvey let in Ross's twin striker and he made it 2-0. Soon after, the whistle went for half-time.

Bob Nelson raced to join the Express players. He pounded each of them on the back. 'Great display, lads. Tripe it says on their backs and you're cooking them to a turn. Whenever they get it, nail them . . .'

There was a crisp 'tut-tut' noise behind Bob. He turned to stare into the scowling face of Dave Sharkey. 'Mr Nelson, I expect discipline from my players and from my other staff.' The words came out like a dressing-down from a very heavy headmaster. 'Express members do not *nail* the opposition. If we win, we wir clean.'

'Just a figure of speech, Dave. We're doing so well I got a bit over-excited.' Bob was nearly grovelling.

Sharkey beckoned him away from the players. 'You're not the only one going over the top. Calm your lad down. He's disturbing the rest of the team.'

Bob swallowed hard but managed to give him a ghost of a nod. Sharkey returned to the stands.

Jossy was winding up a lecture that was very much on the subdued side. 'We're letting them make all the running. Ricky – get going at them. Hustle them. Harvey – pick a man when you throw the ball out. And whatever you do, don't say a dicky bird to Ross. He's having a wobbler.'

The Giants nodded grimly and took to the boards for the final ten-minute period. Ross's wildness had now focused on his team-mates. One of them missed a tackle on Glenn who fed through a ball to Selly. 'Call yourself a rotten defender,' Ross had the boy by the shirt, 'you just waved your leg at him.'

'I'll wave more than my leg at you, Big Mouth,' came the reply. The boy was much stockier than Ross and he had the eyes of a hard case. Ross ran off.

The Giants were now putting things together. Glenn and Selly were finding gaps. With five minutes to go, Glenn scored. It was the final spark to Ross's fuse. Ricky collected a ball in mid-field and Ross went in like a runaway lawn mower. Ricky fell to the boards clutching his shin. The referee moved over purposefully.

'Off! You've been asking for it all the game, my lad. Off!'

The referee raised his arm and pointed to the side-line. Ross opened his mouth as if to blast off again. Instead, he walked head down through the Express team. The Giants watched. Even Harvey kept his mouth shut. Sharkey had come down to the side-line and was now seething near Bob Nelson.

'The disgrace! To my team!' He turned to Bob. 'You egged him on, Nelson.' Ross had now joined them. Sharkey turned on him. 'I'm fining you five pounds, Nelson. I'm also suspending . . .'

Sharkey got no further. It was now the turn of Nelson Senior to demonstrate a bit of fireworks. Bob grabbed Sharkey by the tie. 'Fines, suspensions, stupid *discipline*. I've had about enough of you, Sergeant Major Sharkey. As of now, my son and I are no longer with your team.'

Bob ripped off the Express baseball cap and slung it on the floor. Then he ushered Ross to the dressing-room.

The steam had now gone out of the Express. Some precise passing by the Giants cut them apart. Ricky and Wayne scored. In the end, the Giants won 3-2. Nobody was quite as excited as they should have been except, of course, Mr Simeon Tuttle. He was delighted with the 'investment' that Tracey had talked him into.

'What a great display!' Mr Tuttle was pounding Jossy on the back. 'I can't wait to throw a party for you lads. We'll have pop, hot-dogs, black puddings and tripe by the pound.'

As Mr Tuttle zoomed off in search of the photographer from the *Glipton Bugle*, Ricky stepped up to get the cup. Harvey eased up beside Jossy. 'Please don't let Mr Tuttle continue the sponsorship.'

Jossy winked at him and patted his head. 'Don't worry, sunshine. Tripe is definitely off the menu after today.'

SIX

A couple of days later, the Giants were making the most
of Mr Tuttle's victory feast. Jossy's shop was hung with
streamers and silly string. The Crompton Cup, a riot of
plastic and chrome, glistened near the till. The team
were taking their ease and loading up on goodies –
though very little of Mr Tuttle's famous tripe was being
consumed.

'Come on now, Jossy,' Mr Tuttle held a paper plate
of tripe under Jossy's nose, 'it's best with a smidgeon of
pepper and a really big dollop of vinegar.'

'No thanks, Simeon,' replied Jossy, 'I may talk a load
of tripe but I can't swallow it.'

The boys jeered at this. Jossy stood up, put down a
Coke and let his feelings show. 'Lads, I see this as just a
beginning.' Harvey raised his eyes to the roof. The
Geordie was off again. 'First the Crompton Cup – a
symbol of what we can achieve locally . . .'

'Then tomorrow it's "Look out Europe", kidda,'
Ricky made them all laugh with his version of Jossy's
Geordie accent.

Harvey continued the saga. 'Then next stop, my
hinnies, the World Cup Individual Final in Brazil
at the Maracana Stadium, Glipton Giants versus
Barcelona.'

'And I know who'll have to organise the plane tickets

passports and civic receptions!' The boys laughed at Albert's joke.

The doorbell of the shop clanged and everyone looked at the newcomers. Bob Nelson led the way, overdressed and flashy as usual. From his shiny moccasins to his moustache, he was the picture of trendiness. Ross slid in behind his dad.

'I'd like a quiet word with you, Jossy, if I may.' This was not the normal style of Bob Nelson. Jossy nodded and the two men walked into the back room. Tracey picked up a fresh Tuttle sausage butty and forced it on Ross. Harvey pointedly squirted a stream of yellow silly string at the Crompton Cup.

'I had a good, hard, honest think after the 5-a-side final, Jossy, and I'm thoroughly ashamed of myself.'

The look in Bob's eyes did not quite match the sombreness of the words. Jossy was suspicious. Bob continued: 'It was rotten of me to pile on the pressure. We deserted the club; I took my money out; and I stopped your credit at my betting shop. The actions of a mean-minded man.'

Jossy was thinking, *you said it, pal*, but he said nothing. Bob got to the point. 'In short, Jossy, I come in sackcloth and ashes.' Jossy eyed Bob's knuckleduster rings and medallion. 'I – we – would like to go back to square one.'

When Jossy spoke quietly, which was not often, his Geordie accent was much more pronounced. 'You're not a little laddie now, Bob. Life's not that easy. You and your lad left us in the lurch.'

The Giants kept looking across to the back room dying to know what was going on. The men looked like a couple of fencers not over eager to strike and risk losing balance.

Bob looked rather shifty, then gathered himself together and said, with a lot of effort, 'I want to make amends, Jossy. So I propose that I restore your credit account at my shop. And you can have *unlimited* credit.'

The ice melted out of Jossy's attitude. His blue eyes sparkled with a mixture of hope and pure greed. This was a Geordie chancer's dream come true. Faith could maybe move mountains, but credit at the betting shop could shake up the solar system. He did not take much time to come to a decision.

'I am not an unreasonable man, Bob. Don't think I can be bought – but, well the quality of mercy should not be strained. So, aye, we'll have you both back in the club.'

Bob smiled his most sincere smile. He put his arm around Jossy's shoulders and they went into the shop to join the feast. A thought crossed Jossy's mind. 'I must have been just about your best customer.'

Bob winked. 'Something like that, kidda.'

The two men each grabbed a Tuttle butty and Jossy joined Tracey and Ross. From the looks on the faces of the other Giants, Jossy reckoned that there was no need to formally welcome Ross back to the fold. He was in. But it was not in Jossy's nature to let water flow, under bridges or anything else, without the odd ripple.

'I know you play like Attila the Hun at times, sunshine,' said Jossy, his eyes on the Tuttle butty that Ross was wolfing down, 'but there's no need to adopt his table manners.'

'Same old Jossy,' said Ross with a grin.

'Same old jokes,' replied Tracey.

After the triumph, and the trauma, of the Crompton Cup, Jossy had given the lads a few days off training. But now he was thinking he had been a bit lax. It was five past ten on a Saturday morning; he had called the team for ten sharp – and nobody had turned up. Jossy was just thinking how fickle kids were, when he spotted the lone figure of Harvey McGuinn mooching along the canal towpath practising the odd pirouette.

'Stroll on,' muttered Jossy to himself. 'Here's me trying to organise a team of world-beaters and all I've got to work on is an ice-dance fantasist.'

But when Harvey joined Jossy in the goalmouth it was not his dream subject that was on his mind. It was football. 'Jossy, how many goals did the one and only Jackie Milburn score in his first trial for Newcastle?'

The question took the wind out of Jossy's sails. Could it be that Harvey had at last become a hundred per cent committed to football? Was this an historic moment? His answer was hushed, as if uttered in church.

'Six. He came on the bus from Ashington with his boots in a brown carrier bag. And he nearly burst the net. In fact . . .'

The gush was stopped by Harvey. 'OK, thanks. Next question. What year did Newcastle enter the Football League?' Harvey had now pulled a scrap of paper and a biro from his tracksuit pocket. Jossy was suspicious. He was also ignorant of the particular fact required.

'What do you want to know all this for? Are you having me on?' Jossy glared at Harvey.

'Calm down, Boss. Believe it or not, football is not the only thing in the world.' This piece of home-spun philosophy sounded rich coming from Harvey. But Jossy let him go on. 'Miss Lanchester, our history teacher, has got us all doing projects. You can pick what you like – Ancient Rome, Hannibal's elephant act, First World War, French Revolution, all the aristos going for the chop – anything you like. I'm doing 'The History of Newcastle United' and you're an expert on them aren't you?'

Jossy nodded, slightly flattered but still waiting for the rug to be pulled.

'At least I'm here for the practice.' Harvey sounded very self-righteous and he grinned at Jossy. 'The others are all off digging in libraries, I reckon.'

Just as Harvey spoke, a couple of figures came through the gap in the hedge at the canal end of St James' Park and stood for a while looking at the oak tree. It was Tracey and Ross.

Jossy spotted them. 'Oh, another scholar hot on the trail. But at least wearing a tracksuit.' He raised his voice. 'Hey, Ross, nice of you to drop by. Thinking of practising?'

Ross and Tracey jogged up to them and Tracey pointed back to the tree. 'It's very exciting, Jossy. I'm pretty sure the oak tree was witness to a Civil War battle that raged right where we're standing now.'

'Oh, yes, I can see it now.' It was apparent from Ross's tone that he was not taking the project lark totally seriously. 'Welcome to St James' Park, fans. The score here is Roundheads 2, Cavaliers 2. We're in the last minute of ye extra time for the Oliver Cromwell Challenge Cuppe. John de Motson reporting directly from ye ground.'

'Typical,' sneered Tracey. 'What's your project, Ross?'

As Ross hesitated, Harvey chipped in: 'The Development of Male Fashion from Beau Brummel to Boy George? That would just suit you, Ross.'

Ross was stuck for an answer. Jossy had had enough of patter and history. He began the practice in a novel way. From the pocket of his tracksuit he produced a yellow tennis ball and began playing keepy-uppy with it. As he flicked the ball from foot to foot he explained. 'I used to spend hours like this in the back lane. My mother used to bring my tea out to me. Dedicated I was.'

Ten minutes later the rest of the Giants were paying patchy attention to the demonstration of basic ball skills. Ricky was the most enthusiastic. He began flipping the ball with his foot and even managed a couple of headers.

'Hey, it's great this, Boss. My dad says that Don Bradman used to smack a golf ball against a tree with a cricket stump for hours.'

'Exactly,' Jossy was delighted to have at least one disciple. 'Playing with a tennis ball sharpens up your reflexes.'

Jossy formed them into a circle around him and began flicking the tennis ball at their heads. Harvey was not really entering into the spirit of things. He made several half-hearted attempts to head the ball, then sat down in disgust.

'This is a farce. Tennis balls, golf balls. You'll have us practising with snooker balls next.'

Ross, who was now enjoying the game, had a go at Harvey. 'If this bores you so much, why don't you slip off to the ice rink and practise a few pirouettes?'

'Yeah, get the girls to help you into your funky leotard, man,' added Ricky.

It was all too much for Harvey. Red faced, he marched off. But he could not resist one last over-the-shoulder crack. 'I'll show you lot. There's some ice-dancing auditions coming up soon and I'm going to star in them.'

Ross stopped kicking the tennis ball. He looked at Jossy. 'One of these days, Boss, that lad is going to have to put his skates where his mouth is.'

'*Can* he skate?' asked Jossy.

'Who knows?' said Ricky.

'And don't you need a partner to ice-dance?' Ross looked amused.

Later that day an excited group of Giants, minus Harvey who was still in a huff with them, was gathered in Jossy's shop. At last the *Glipton Bugle* was slipped through the door and Albert was delegated to read out the great deeds of the Crompton Cup triumph.

'Now, don't scoff you lot! Here we go.' Albert worked a bit of the Robin Days into his Mancunian accent. 'The Glipton Giants deservedly won the Crompton Cup 5-a-side tournament staged at the Community Centre . . .'

Jossy broke in: 'Don't read the lot, Albert, just the juicy bits.'

Albert scanned the column. He paused and rather archly looked at Jossy before reading the next bit. 'Throughout the tournament the Giants were urged on by their ebullient manager, Mr Joswell Blair . . .'

A tidal wave of jeers greeted this. Jossy went purple. Ross's voice rose above the din. 'What's ebullient mean, Boss?'

Jossy looked sharp but then doubt clouded his face. He looked at Tracey and began to hedge.

'Well, it's kind of . . .'

'Bouncy. Breezy.' Tracey saved his blushes. There were odd jeers of 'never' from the lads.

Ross stepped in. 'When I've read it in books it means, brash, brazen or boastful.'

'It'll do me,' said Jossy with a wink. 'Read on, McDuff.'

Albert had scarcely started the next juicy bit when Daz and Dean, two eight-year-old urchins who had become self-appointed mascots of the team, raced in the door. Daz's red hair was all over the place and his freckled face was flushed with excitement. He addressed his remarks to Ricky. 'It's Harvey. He's down the ice rink. He says he's going to ice-dance. A lad there sent us to get you. He says nobody here has ever seen him skate.'

There was a stunned silence. Jossy broke it with a murmur. 'Harvey goes to hospital. Come on gang.' As the team raced out, Jossy turned to Tracey. 'There's a whole new pile of mail came in the past few weeks, Tracey. Fancy doing a bit of admin?'

Tracey nodded. She knew where the paperwork would be 'filed'. The briefcase was in its usual place by the till. She opened it and found the latest bills and the other unopened letters at the bottom. One of the letters was from the council. It was postmarked a month past. Tracey opened the envelope, pulled out the letter and began to read. Gradually her usually firm jaw dropped slacker and slacker.

To Harvey the scene was crystal clear. Vivid, purple-tinged lights swept the ice like passing clouds. Powerful musical chords rang out into the chilly night. Several thousand gasps became a roar as a lone figure in a spangled leotard began a series of delicate maneouvres on the ice. The voice of Alan Weekes, hushed in wonder, relayed the experience to millions of viewers. 'A sight to gladden the heart of everyone in Britain. This young man, Harvey McGuinn of Glipton, skating with a cool-ness that belies his lack of years. I have rarely seen elegance and control like it.'

'Six point nought. Six point nought. Six point nought.' Harvey was still reciting out loud as he came out of his daydream. The purple leotard his mum had bought him and his skates were real enough, but the Glipton Icedrome was more like a disused Zeppelin hanger than an Olympic rink. Also, his skating needed a bit of work before he could really seriously go hunting for medals. He could do all sorts of tricks in straight lines but he could not turn to save his life.

Reality surged in on Harvey even stronger as he heard some familiar voices echoing from the entrance to the spectator's gallery. 'Come on lads. Harvey must still be in the changing rooms. Wait till he gets out there and realises he's got an audience.' It was Ross's voice. It made Harvey's stomach churn. He would show them. He hunched down further below the barrier near the ice.

It was a dream of glory, still bright in his brain, that tipped the scales. The 'Bolero' music starting up on the tannoy helped. Like a robot blowing all its fuses, Harvey launched himself on to the ice. He tried the lot; a jump, a spin, and a one-legged glide. For exactly thirty seconds it all miraculously worked. Not a jeer escaped from the lips of any Giant. Then Harvey whizzed off the ice and landed in a heap amongst the remains of a cardboard castle from last year's 'Extravaganza on Ice.'

Jossy leapt to his feet. 'He can do it!'

'Up to a point,' said Ross.

They all rushed to pick Harvey up. He did not even notice the new light of respect in their eyes. Jossy was pounding him on the back as if he had just saved a decisive penalty.

'You were conning us all the time! You can skate like a dream.'

'But I can't turn,' Harvey bleated.

'It'll come, son, it'll come.'

Nobody had noticed Tracey, who was now standing by the edge of the ice with a piece of paper in her hand. Her solemn face held a message. They crowded round her. She held up the letter and looked hard at Jossy.

'This is a letter from Glipton Council. It was delivered to your shop one month ago, Jossy. It says that a group of developers have permission to turn Canalside Stadium – our stadium – into a supermaket. The demolition work will begin on Saturday. I've checked at the Council offices and they confirm everything.'

SEVEN

Once again the Glipton Giants were in the jaws of a crisis. Jossy, Tracey and Albert had read and re-read the Council's letter and the fact had to be faced: St James' Park was to be obliterated from soccer history in a few days' time.

The Giants hung dolefully round in Jossy's shop. Ricky and Ross bashed a set of pool balls around a table listlessly. Tracey and Albert mooched about as if stock-taking. They both knew what the ground closure would mean – the look on Jossy's face said it all. Once the bulldozers rolled, his dream would die and the Glipton Giants would disintegrate.

Fortunately some of the lads were not to know this. A weird pair walked through the door. Glenn was wearing a German soldier's 'bucket' hat and had a ceremonial SS dagger in a sheath fastened to a belt round his trousers. Selly's blue hair splayed out from under an officer's cap and he almost tripped as the sword he had on tangled with his legs. Normally there would have been derisive remarks about the 'Kaiser Bill' look, but not today.

'It's no time for jokes.' Tracey's remark should have put them both down.

The hackles rose on Glenn and Selly. Both normally kow-towed to Tracey because they fancied as well as respected her. But today they were on their mettle.

71

'This lot is part of our history project! We're studying the German Third Reich,' said Selly.

'And it gave us an idea.' Everybody looked at Glenn, whose ideas normally went no further than a safety-pin through a nostril. 'Well, the Germans thought they could do what they liked. Thought they could walk over everybody. But people resisted!'

'That's what we should do,' added Selly. 'Resist the Council. Protest! *Fight*!'

The remark ignited Jossy's blue touchpaper. His face glowed with pride. He embraced Glenn and Selly like a French general greeting heroes back from the front. 'That's what I call the Giant spirit! Here we are sitting like birds in the wilderness, stewing – and brains have been working on our behalf. I think that Glenn and Selly deserve a round of applause.'

Jossy waited but no applause came. There were, however, a lot of eager faces. 'Right,' shouted Jossy, 'as Napoleon said to the lads – *Aux arms, citoyens.*'

'Look what happened to Napoleon,' murmured Ricky.

'Yeah,' said Ross, 'they gave him the Elba.'

The streets of Glipton had never seen anything like it. A little bit of what the peaceful citizens watched nightly on the television news had come to their streets – almost. And weird and wonderful were the forms that the 'Save St James' Park' campaign took.

Little Daz, clad from top to toe in black and white, came out of an alley and into the main street. He held high a placard with the slogan 'Hands off the Giants' ground'. People stared at this grim-faced, goose-stepping kid. Down the alley his friend Dean, who was only eight, was being briefed on his task. Glenn and Selly had given him a placard saying, 'Support Local Soccer', that Selly had lettered and they were priming him with sweets. 'Go as far as the "Turk's Head", then

cross the street. Then come back here. Understood?'
Glenn was a bit worried that Dean's mind was more on
fruit pastilles than protest but these were the best
'troops' they had.

'I want hard gums when I get back,' mumbled Dean
between chews.

'I'll give you loose gums if you don't get marching.'
Selly pushed the kid out into the street.

Glenn adjusted a couple of the spikes of his Mohican,
coloured alternate black and white for the protest. Selly
had not gone quite so far. He had borrowed a motorbike
leather jacket from a soul mate and painted an enormous
Magpie on the back. They both took ends of a banner
that read 'Punks for Posterity. Support the Giants.' Off
they went into the street, chains clanking and Docs
stomping.

Moving in the opposite direction, on the other side of
the street, were Albert and Jossy. The gear they were
sporting was certainly attracting attention. Albert was
tricked out in a Newcastle United strip of the 1920s,
string fastening at the throat, long shorts and the kind of
boots that could crush cement. He pushed a pram
containing Jossy, who had really gone over the top.
Clad in his tracksuit, he was clutching the German
sword that appeared to be stuck in his chest. Odd
moans drifted from his throat as he pointed pathetically
to a placard that read, 'Victim of Town Hall Dictateor-
ship'.

A bloke walked out of the 'Turk's Head' and looked
at both of them. He dug in his pocket and slipped Albert
a fifty pence piece. He pointed to Jossy. 'Take him to
Blackpool, mate. They'll love him at the Chamber of
Horrors.'

After an hour of parading up and down, the Giants
and their supporters called it a day. They were all
bemoaning the local apathy to their problem when

Tracey showed up looking a lot more bouncy than they did. She made straight for Jossy. 'You didn't tell me you had friends in high places.'

'Oh, I do?' Jossy did not know how to take it.

'Have you got a–er – largish lady in your keep-fit class?'

Jossy puzzled for a second. Then he twigged. 'Strapping blonde lassie. Miss Fletcher?'

'*Councillor* Fletcher.' Tracey's voice was full of significance. 'Chairperson of the Sports and Leisure Committee. Mind you she doesn't look a model of fitness to me.' Jossy gave her an impatient look. She continued: 'Well, I had a brainwave. I went down to the Town Hall and I explained our desperate position to Miss Fletcher. I laid it on really thick. 'Death of a dream', all that bit. Oh what a-sighing and a-sobbing there would be. And she said, once she heard *you* were involved, that she just might be able to use her influence on our behalf.'

'That's great Tracey.' Jossy was impressed. 'Do you reckon I should step in now and give her a bit of the old Geordie charm?'

There was something not a hundred per cent certain in Tracey's eyes. 'Councillor Fletcher says that she would like to see you at her house at seven tomorrow night.'

Jossy was knocked back at this. 'Why can't I just toddle down to the council offices to see her?'

'Because the Councillor says at her house so her house it's going to be. And you'll have to smarten up your act.'

Jossy had a lot of help in getting ready for his date with Councillor Fletcher. The Giants knew that he was not by nature a ladies' man, so they were trying every trick in the book to enhance his appeal. What they had to work on was not exactly perfect material.

Half an hour before he was due at the Councillor's house Jossy stood in the shop with some of the Giants. He was wearing a suit whose style was ancient when Cliff Richard was still a lad. It was lovat green and had narrow lapels and wide trouser bottoms. His shirt was pink with a deep pointed collar.

Ross was the first to try his hand at jazzing up Jossy's image. He pulled from his pocket a tie like an explosion in a paint factory and tried to knot it round Jossy's neck.

'It would look smarter if you fastened the top button of your shirt,' said Ross.

Jossy wrestled to oblige. He succeeded in getting the button fastened then found he had great difficulty moving his head in any direction. 'The last time I wore a tie was at my Uncle Barney's funeral in Gateshead ten years ago,' he gasped.

As Ross stepped back to admire his handiwork, Ricky pulled up a chair and stood on it behind Jossy. He took a tube from his pocket and began plastering Brylcreem all over Jossy's thinning blond locks. Jossy grinned and bore it. But Glenn's suggestion for even more male glamour was too much.

Glenn had an aerosol spray poised.

'Hey, hang on,' yelled Jossy. 'What's that?'

'Just a drop of green glitter. A couple of streaks will set you off a treat.'

'The Councillor will think I'm a Christmas tree, not a football manager. No, enough is enough.'

The boys stepped back. Tracey edged forward holding a red carnation. She pinned it on Jossy's lapel and popped a delicate kiss on his right cheek. Jossy's blush completed the clashing range of colours. He bore a strong resemblance to a stick of rock.

Tracey was not finished. She took a large white handkerchief from her pocket and folded it neatly. She tucked it into Jossy's breast pocket. Leaning forward, she whispered, 'If you panic and need to make a strategic withdrawal, wave this.'

Jossy looked worried. 'I know that I have to get round to asking for her help. But I ought to lead up to it. How will I know when to make my plea?'

Tracey plastered down one last wayward lock of hair. 'Be your usual charming self and there'll be no trouble. We'll advise you stage by stage.'

Jossy was about to ask more about this but Tracey urged him towards the door.

'Bye, gang,' said Jossy.

'Bye, Boss,' came the reply.

It did not seem to bother anyone that he had forgotten a bunch of mixed flowers that a band of volunteers had nicked from the park.

Councillor Glenda Fletcher did not hold much truck with the modern ideas of Women's Lib. She was what a less sophisticated age called a 'man eater'. If a gentleman came calling, he would find Glenda with her stall well and truly set out. Tonight was just such a night. Her maisonette was as glossy and bright as a showhouse. A coffee table was set with a bottle of wine and two glasses, in front of a brightly-chintzed settee. Glenda plumped the cushions, dipped into the kitchen to check on proceedings there and adjusted the fine detail of her beehive hairdo in the mirror. The doorbell was due to ring any time. As a last touch she opened the windows to the garden, letting a welcome breath of fresh October air into the overheated atmosphere.

The doorbell announced the arrival of Jossy. Glenda swept to let him in. Jossy looked like a kid who had come round to borrow a cup of sugar.

'Good evening Mr Blair,' Glenda gushed.

Jossy stretched out his hand to shake hers as he had

seen people do in movies. Glenda hauled him inside. She led him to the settee by the open window. There was a snorting and sniffing noise from outside.

'Shall I close the window?' asked Glenda.

'Oh no!' Jossy almost panicked. 'Us sporty types need bags of fresh air.' He began taking deep breaths until the knot of his tie made him turn red.

Glenda snuggled close up to him on the settee. 'Yes. I had you marked down as a keep-fit fanatic by the way you took our ladies' aerobics class. And I think Jossy is such a lovely name. Strong, lyrical, with a dash of the flavour of the Northumbrian moors. I know them well. I went walking there often as a girl.' Glenda stood up sharply. 'I have a few little titbits in the oven. Would you excuse me?'

'Oh yes, by all means. A drop of scoff would slip down a treat.'

As Glenda went out, there was a rustling at the window. Jossy turned to see a black balaclava helmet with two eyes handing him the bunch of flowers. It spoke in Ross's voice. 'You forgot these!' The apparition ducked back down. Glenda came back.

'I hope you'll accept a few posies.'

Glenda did a double take at the sudden appearance of the flowers. But she accepted them all the same.

'I hope you're not too fitness conscious to accept a glass of wine, Jossy?'

'No, love. A drop of plonk is OK by me.'

As Glenda turned her attention to pouring the drinks, Jossy's eyes strayed to the window. Five black balaclavas with eyeholes stared back at him. All five gave him the thumbs up. He decided to proceed to business.

'Councillor . . .' Jossy began.

'Glenda!'

'Glenda. Now I don't want you to get the impression that I'm abrupt –' she handed him a glass and he took a minute sip – 'but can you help us stop the developers wrecking our ground on Saturday?'

Glenda twirled her glass with her fingers and put on a very important voice. 'As Chairwoman of a key committee I can certainly exert pressure. But, more directly, there is a certain document –' there was a gasp from the garden – 'in the council archives that could possibly change the whole situation.'

Seeing she had Jossy hooked, Glenda changed course for a while. 'Let's discuss the document after we've had a few nibbles, shall we?'

'Anything you like, love.' Jossy was feeling peckish.

As soon as Glenda's back was turned, a head bobbed up at the window. It was Tracey. 'When you get a chance, try to persuade her to get the document out of the archives for us to look at.'

Before Jossy could ask how he was doing so far, Tracey bobbed down. Glenda appeared from the kitchen with a tray of food.

'I've eaten earlier, myself. But I thought you might like quiche, vol-au-vents and sorbet to follow.'

Jossy managed a weak grin. He was normally a meat pie and mushy peas man. Glenda put down the tray and turned to the stereo. 'A little music, Jossy?'

'Oh, yes.'

Quick as a flash, Jossy lifted the tray of food to the window, where eager hands scooped off the contents. He wiped a pretend crumb from his mouth as Glenda turned back to him and goggled at the empty tray.

'Hungry work this football management, love.'

The look in Glenda's eye was now very definitely romantic. She sat down very close to Jossy.

'Tell me more about this document that could help us.'

'I occasionally dabble into local history. More than once I have come across references to the Moreton

78

Manuscript. It's very old, apparently, and in parts almost illegible, but it does give details of a battle. Most authorities agree that during the Civil War a battle was fought in or around Canal Fields . . .'

'You mean where our ground is?'

'Precisely.' Glenda sipped more of her wine. 'General Humphrey Moreton, who lost the battle, was a local landowner. It's said that he escaped, having hidden once the game was up.'

'Smart lad,' said Jossy.

'I must stress that all this conjecture. I am no expert. But the Moreton Manuscript *could* prove that your ground is of historical importance.'

Jossy paused, screwing up his courage to make the fateful move. 'Could you possibly let us have access to the document?'

Glenda jolted forward, almost spilling her wine. 'But that – for a person in my position – would be like divulging a state secret.'

Jossy detected that Glenda's outrage was not quite genuine. He tried whimsy. 'Well, we're in a right state – and that's no secret.'

Glenda's eyes lit up with merriment. 'Not only a thorough charmer, but witty too.'

A burst of laughter filtered in from the garden. Jossy whipped in. 'Sounds like you've got rats in the garden!' To distract her, Jossy looked deep into Glenda's eyes. He gave her a little-boy-lost look. 'If you could manage to sneak the manuscript out for a bit, I'd be eternally grateful, Glenda.'

Glenda leaned her head ever so gently against Jossy's chest. He turned crimson.

'Here, love. My tummy's still rumbling. You don't think you could rustle me up a condensed milk sandwich do you – kind of as a pudding?'

Glenda jumped to attention. 'If that's what you'd like.'

79

Jossy burbled on. 'My mam used to make them for me when I was a laddie. She'd bring them out into the back lane during our marathon football games.' He closed his eyes and wallowed in nostalgia. 'Heaven – a condensed milk sandwich and a glass of Vimto.'

Glenda could not manage the Vimto. But Jossy wolfed down the sandwich in four bites.

'Delicious,' he said, 'every bit as good as my mam's.'

Glenda now moved in for the kill. She snuggled up to Jossy and began to stroke his tie. It was crisis point. Jossy arched away from Glenda, pulled the handkerchief out of his breast pocket and began mopping his brow extravagantly. This was the danger signal.

'My, it's hot in here, love.' Jossy walked over to the window and waved the handkerchief wildly. Glenda manoeuvred him back on to the settee.

'You must tell me about your early life on Tyneside. Was your family very poor?'

Jossy stood up. 'Poor? I'll say. I remember once we had to pawn my grannie's false teeth for a week.'

'Oh, Jossy, what a tease you are.'

The phone rang and Jossy was on it in a flash. His face screwed up with concern.

'A what? A break-in? At my shop. I don't believe it! I'll be round there right away.'

Glenda jumped to her feet. Jossy put the phone down.

'Oh, what awful news, Jossy!'

'Can't be helped. I'll have to get down there quick though. I'll send Tracey, my right-hand lassie, round to the Town Hall to have a look at that Moreton Manuscript, OK?'

Jossy moved towards the door. Glenda followed. She looked as though she was expecting a kiss. Jossy gave her a stiff handshake. 'Goodnight, Glenda.'

'Goodnight, Jossy. Do drop in any time.' There was a

note of disappointment in the voice.

Five minutes later Jossy met the gang at the phone box.

'Thanks a million, Tracey. It was getting pretty steamy in there.'

'You were lapping it up,' said Tracey icily.

'All for a good cause,' said Jossy with a slow wink.

EIGHT

Harvey McGuinn was really down in the dumps. He had been ploughing his straight, lonely furrow up and down and across the ice rink for an hour and the staff were starting to put the lights out. His balance had been great throughout the session but he could still not turn. 'Maybe if I imagine I had a partner, the turn would come naturally.' Harvey closed his eyes, raised his arms as if clutching a real partner and leaned into a graceful curve. The crash echoed to the rafters as he thudded down on to the ice.

'Keep trying!'

Tracey had been watching him from the edge of the rink. Harvey scrambled to his feet and joined her.

'There's not much wrong with your balance. But I think your weight's wrong when you go into the turn. I might be able to help you if you give me a hand with a job I've got.'

'You – help!' Harvey saw a spark of light in his life. 'Can you skate?'

'Oh yes. And I can ice-dance too. Look, even though your mind's on the skating, you do want to help us fight the bulldozers don't you?'

Harvey nodded vigorously. He was not that much in love with football but he liked being one of the Giants.

'I've just been to see Councillor Glenda Fletcher, who Jossy softened up the other night. She's going to let me look at an historical document down the Reading Room at the Town Hall. It could help us save our ground. But if I'm to go through it in two days flat and check the references properly, I need an assistant. Are you on?'

Harvey did not need to think. When he put his mind to schoolwork he was good and Tracey knew this. He nodded agreement.

After school the next day, Tracey and Harvey walked down the echoey marble corridors of Glipton Town Hall. The brass on the stair-rails shone like new, and ancient worthies of the textile trade with names like Absalom Crabtree and George Henry Blount, glowered down at them. Even before they got to the Reading Room, the musty atmosphere brought on Harvey's hay fever. His loud sneezing upset a few of the regulars, even though most of them were studying either the racing pages or *The Dalesman*.

Harvey was most impressed by the dark oak panelling of the Reading Room and Tracey had a job to drag him away from the exhibits of Glipton memorabilia displayed in glass cabinets. There were old clogs, old prints and even an old school bell.

'Trust you and your butterfly mind,' whispered Tracey, 'I drag you down here to do a job and you start acting like a junior antiquarian.'

She pulled a large magnifying glass out of her school hold-all. Pointing to the Glipton local history section, she gave Harvey a list of reference books to collect. They had arranged to meet Councillor Glenda Fletcher, now she walked down the room holding an old parchment book as if it were the Ark of the Covenant. Tracey turned on the charm.

'So good of you to help us, Councillor. You must be so busy.'

Glenda looked suitably pompous. She placed the

ancient book down on a green baize-topped table. The silk of her dress ruffled as she held herself erect.

'Mr Blair said you were a most reliable, conscientious girl, Tracey. So I know you'll handle the Moreton Manuscript with the utmost care. In fact, I think white gloves . . .'

Tracey produced a pair from her hold-all. 'My dad's a snooker referee,' she said – as a joke.

'I don't like the game. Young people should be out of doors, not draped over tables in a half light.'

Tracey did not dispute this. Glenda looked at her watch as Harvey joined them, loaded down with books.

'I'm off to a meeting now. Be sure to hand the manuscript back to the librarian before you leave. I wish you lots of luck with your researches.'

Two hours later Tracey, patches of dust all over her gloves and face, was realising what a mammoth task she had taken on. The parchment was very dark brown and in places the ink simply merged into the page. Harvey had had very little to do. But when Tracey came across a crude sketch map of the Glipton area in the seventeenth century, things began to warm up. She managed to decipher some of the words below the map.

'It says that the battle began at a cleft in a flat-topped moor. So, Harvey, look in the Gazeteer for place names featuring the word "moor".'

Harvey's eyes were streaming from the dust but he waded through the book. 'Littlemoor. Uppermoor. Danesmoor – too early. Here, how about Clough Moor – that's where the golf club is . . .'

'. . . and you can see it from our ground.' Tracey was now on the track like a ferret. She peered through the magnifying glass at the ancient text. Her voice became very excited. 'General Moreton withdrew his troops over a moss and the fighting was thickest round some oak trees where grazed the local swine.' Tracey was flying. 'Moss meant marsh in those days, I think. So look up marsh land.'

After a couple of minutes Harvey found something. 'It says here that marshland formed the northern boundary of Sir Humphrey Moreton's land . . .'

'So Canal Fields is the marshland where the battle was thickest.' Tracey was delighted.

An attendant came up on them quietly and reminded them that the Reading Room was shortly closing for the night. That gave them only one more day to uncover something in the Moreton Manuscript.

'Back again tomorrow,' said Tracey, as they went down the Town Hall steps.

'What about my hay fever?' asked Harvey.

'Bring a gas mask,' was Tracey's parting shot.

Albert Hanson had been racking his brains all day about ways to prevent the demolition of St James' Park. Now he was walking home from his job in the Accounts Department of Whitley's mill and his mind was a blank. Jossy had called an emergency meeting of all the lads at his shop at seven o'clock so there was just time for Albert to have his tea, a read of the evening paper and a little nap. A piercing whistle stopped him short as he passed the 'Turk's Head' pub on the opposite side of the street.

'Hey, Albert, come on over here. I want to talk to you,' shouted Jossy.

As Albert crossed the road there was the sound of bolts being drawn and Arthur the landlord, no stranger to Albert or Jossy, opened the pub door. In a second Jossy had bundled Albert into the tap room.

'Oh, a fine reputation you'll get us two! Waiting outside the pub at opening time. I've heard of "early doors" but this is ridiculous.' Albert came to his main point. 'And I haven't had my tea.'

'Have some pork scratchings then.' Jossy ordered a packet and two pints of bitter. He led Albert to a corner table.

'I couldn't take the waiting any longer.' Jossy sipped at the ale. 'I thought me and you better have a preliminary chat about the crisis. Maybe by talking it over we can come up with some hope to offer the lads when we see them later.'

Albert munched the scratchings and mumbled, 'I think it's a bit late for hope.'

Jossy realised that Albert was not going to be a great deal of inspiration. Idly his eyes strayed over the pub. There was a moth-eaten dartboard, a crib table and, on the mantelpiece a set of dusty pewter mugs. Above these were one or two old photographs. Jossy got up and paced to the wall. He looked up at the photographs. They were of Second World War scenes: troop landings, aircraft and General Eisenhower shaking hands with Winston Churchill. What a pair of great men, thought Jossy. Churchill! The Bulldog Breed. He twigged what must be done.

Arthur the landlord was in the other bar.

'Arthur. Arthur!' Jossy's yell brought Arthur running, and even lifted Albert's nose from the scratchings. 'Give me the biggest cigar you've got.'

Arthur handed over a large half-corona with a puzzled look. 'Really decided to play the football manager, eh Jossy?'

Jossy took the cigar and pushed it, unwrapped, into his mouth. 'No, Arthur, warlord is more like it.'

The lads thought Jossy had taken leave of his senses when he walked into the shop waving the cigar. Ross was nearest the door and he caught the whiff of beer from Albert's breath.

'I don't believe it. They're both cracking up – taking to drinking and smoking!'

Jossy shot his cuffs and balanced the cigar, now unwrapped, in the 'V' of his fingers. He began to speak in a Churchillian growl. 'Never – in the field of human conflict have I . . .' The strain was too much. He lapsed back into Geordie . . . 'seen so many miserable, defeated faces.'

He looked around at them. The question was aimed at Ricky. 'What did the Trojans do when they saw the wooden horse cantering up to their walls?'

'Knowing you,' said Ricky, 'you'd have put a quid each way on it.'

Jossy refused to be dampened. 'I'll tell you what the Trojans did. They had a siege. They resisted the aggressor! And that's just what we're going to do. We shall turn St James' Park into a fortress.' He went back into his Churchill impression. 'We shall fight them on the touch-lines and on the terraces, on the land and on the sea. Who's with me?'

Jossy scanned his troops with an eagle eye, pacing up and down like a real general. Tracey didn't have the heart to point out that Jossy had got the Trojan Horse story totally wrong. He pointed at Harvey, still splotched with dust from the Reading Room and still emitting the odd explosive sneeze.

'How's the research going?'

'Slow. Bits of info here, bits there. But she won't give up.' said Harvey.

'I'm detaching you from Reading Room duty here and now. I'm going to give you a special assignment.'

Harvey stood to attention. As usual he had his own harumscarum idea. 'I'll be Minister of Supply. Pop, crisps, butties, sweets.'

'No, Harvey old son, I've got something special lined up for you in this campaign. You will be in charge of weapons and ammunition. Smoke bombs, flour bombs, water cannon . . .'

'Water cannon!' Harvey was nonplussed, but not for long. 'I know, my dad's got an old stirrup pump.'

'That's the idea, son.' Jossy turned to Albert.

'Albert. You will head up a special section for Espionage and Disinformation.'

'What's that exactly?' asked Albert.

'Spying and lying,' piped up Ross.

'Correct!' said Jossy.

There was a buzz of excitement amongst the Giants now. Jossy pointed at Glenn and Selly.

'You two will be in charge of camouflage. It can be as way-out as you like. Yellow and black zig-zags on the hardware – sky blue pink on the manpower.'

Glenn's eyes rolled as he thought of the battery of aerosol sprays he could bring into play.

'Ross!'

'Aye, aye, *mon Géneral*,' barked Ross with an extravagant salute.

'Supreme Allied Commander to you, sunshine. You will be in charge of Troop Morale and Propaganda.'

Ross was on the ball in a flash. 'You mean rousing tunes to keep the lads' spirits high. Food parcels for the front. Concert parties, bright lights . . .'

'That kind of thing,' said Jossy. 'Ricky! You will be Minister of Defence. We want barbed wire, bricks – everything from sandbags to beanbags.'

'I'll put it through my computer. It'll be just like Star Wars.' Ricky's normally dour face was glowing.

Jossy turned to the blackboard. He picked up a pool cue and a piece of chalk. Five minutes later the blackboard was covered in arrows as he began outlining his plan of campaign. He tapped the pool cue on a big block at one end of the ground. 'The enemy will approach from the east. We will wait until we see the red of his bloodshot eyes. Then we will pounce. Then . . .'

Harvey jumped up and saluted. He was obviously

enjoying this. 'Permission to speak, sir.'

'Speak,' said Jossy.

'Can I go off now and do some recruiting?'

'Certainly, Sergeant McGuinn. Dismissed.'

The countdown to the Siege of St James' Park started at six o'clock on Saturday morning. Harvey had had a tough job rousing Daz and Dean, his eight-year-old 'recruits', by chucking gravel at their bedroom windows. They had both, however, been startled into wakefulness once they set their sleepy eyes on Harvey's attire. His mum was a big wheel in the Glipton Amateur Operatic Society and she had let Harvey loose in the costume store. The result was a weird mixture; a three-cornered Long John Silver type hat, a Chelsea Pensioner's coat, khaki puttees and a pair of shoes with bright silver buckles.

Harvey was now pushing his dad's old wooden wheelbarrow along the shale track to St James' Park. It contained every known kind of mucky bomb, including some 'soot specials'. On top of these was a selection of old fencing, barbed wire and a rusty old stirrup pump.

'Hey, wait for us Harvey.' Daz and Dean, both camouflaged and face-blackened, had been on the forage. They had 'borrowed' an old hose pipe and were now lugging it along the path. Harvey stopped until they caught up with him and chucked the hose pipe on the barrow.

On the other side of the canal, a suspicious-looking figure dressed all in black was lurking by the junction of the main road and the tarmac road to the ground. Two determined eyes peered out of a black balaclava, scanning the highway for a sign of police cars. Then Albert did his 007 bit.

A rickety signpost pointed the way to Canalside Stadium, with St James' Park scrawled underneath in felt pen. Albert took hold of the signpost and worked it out of the ground. Then he pitched it into the hedge bottom. It was little more than a gesture but at least it made him feel good.

The Number 44 bus from Glipton to Wasley had seen some strange sights, particularly when the pubs closed on Saturday nights, but today's sight was a purler. Jossy appeared from the stairs and walked along the top deck in a Rommel outfit: leather boots, riding trousers, shiny leather belts and a Panzer hat with a skull and crossbones badge. A monocle was squeezed between his nose and the top of his right eye.

'Morning ladies,' he said as he passed down the aisle.

The two shoppers stared and mumbled something about the growing number of nutters in the locality. The conductor had tattoos and generally bore strong evidence of an Elvis Presley fetish. 'Where to General? The Somme, Austerlitz, or will you settle for Waterloo?'

'Field Marshall to you, petal, Ten pence. And easy on the backchat or I'll send the Gestapo round.' Jossy stared fixedly ahead as he had seen George C. Scott do in 'Patton – Lust for Glory.'

The conductor rapped out the ticket. 'Going to collect a medal are we, or are you doing it for a bet?'

Jossy's reply was quiet and firm. 'No. As a matter of fact I'm going to start a war.'

'You've got a nice day for it.' The conductor made a screwing motion with his finger to his temple as he passed the lady shoppers. They moved another half-dozen seats away from Jossy.

The bulldozers were due to rumble at noon. By half-past eleven the Giants' answer to the Maginot Line was almost complete on the half-way line of St James' Park. For twenty yards either side of the centre spot ran a four-foot high wall of sandbags, sacks full of stones, bricks and old fencing. Barbed wire had been stuck on top of this. Ricky was bellowing at Daz and Dean, who were sweating like beach donkeys, to build up the middle of the wall where 'General Blair' would do his Horatio act. Ricky was wearing a baggy *Dad's Army* outfit and a tin hat.

'On the double you two. General Blair will do a wobbly if this wall isn't finished.'

Ross had not gone as far over the top with the military look as others. In fact he managed to look positively trendy in 'back from Vietnam' fatigues and a bush cap. He staggered up to the troops carrying an old-fashioned gramophone and a pile of records. Seeing that he was not camouflaged, Glenn and Selly waylaid him, blackened his face and daubed green paint on his vest. Ross did not protest.

'How long have your men been working?' Ross asked Ricky and Harvey.

'Since dawn.'

'Right,' said Ross, 'they'll need some rousing music.'

He set up the gramophone and soon the strains of 'Keep Right on to the End of the Road' were echoing scratchily round the ground. Daz and Dean clapped their hands to their ears and ran over.

'What's that rubbish?'

'Rubbish!' yelled Ross. 'It's meant to set the blood pounding in your veins.'

'It's awful,' said Dean. 'Ain't you got no Springsteen?'

With fifteen minutes to go, the last bit of the defences – an old pram – was placed on the wall. Harvey issued his final order to Daz and Dean. 'Right, men. Break out the heavy weaponry.'

The kids dragged out the stirrup pump with the hose-pipe attached and an odd-looking wooden contraption that looked like a see-saw.

Ross sneered at it. 'What *is* that?'

'A little trick I picked up from the Romans. Observe.' Harvey placed a flour bomb on one end of the catapult. He told Daz to stand at the other end. Albert was lurking in his black spy gear. Harvey beckoned him over.

'Go and stand about ten yards into No-Man's Land will you, Albert?'

'What for?' asked Albert.

'An exercise in ballistics.'

As Albert marched off, the rest of the troops crowded round the catapult. Harvey gave Daz the nod and he jumped on the raised end. The flour bomb whizzed through the air to burst on Albert's balaclava. The Giants cheered.

'A direct hit,' yelled Harvey.

Ross noticed Jossy striding purposefully from behind the grandstand. He put 'Colonel Bogey' on the gramophone. The troops instinctively formed a line behind the wall. The music put a spring in Jossy's step. He eyed them through his monocle.

'Stand by for full inspection, men.'

The group stood to attention. Suddenly Glenn and Selly stepped forward.

'Permission to camouflage the Commanding Officer, sir?' asked Glenn.

'Permission granted. Proceed.'

Jossy stood like Sitting Bull before a big fight as Glenn and Selly gave him the paint and twig treatment. He glowered Daz and Dean to silence when they got the giggles. Soon the inspection began.

Jossy seemed well pleased by the turn-out. He stopped at Ricky who was last in the line. 'A fine job you've made of that wall, Sweet.'

There was a low roar from behind the grandstand and a pair of bulldozers came slowly into view.

Ricky murmured softly, 'Time to see just how secure

our defences really are – sir.'

Jossy looked round, then turned back to the parade. His voice trembled as he spoke. 'This is it, fellas.' The Siege of St James' Park. Whatever happens, let it always be said, "They did their best". Man the barricades.'

They all rushed to their positions as the two bull-dozers trundled nearer, followed by a flash car with dark-tinted windows. The bulldozers pulled up ten yards from the wall. The car stayed further back.

The bulldozers revved up menacingly. Jossy climbed to the top of the wall by the pram. He dropped his arm. A barrage of flour, soot and water bombs flew at the bulldozers. The stirrup pump was aimed and spread the mush all over the windscreens. The bulldozers stopped. Two burly drivers got out and methodically cleared a patch to see through. One shook his head sadly and got back in.

'We'll never give up,' shouted Jossy as Ross put 'There'll Always be an England' on the gramophone. This time the bulldozers came to within five yards of the wall and stopped.

'Why aren't you firing?' Jossy yelled to nobody in particular.

Harvey presented a sad face. 'Catapult and manual bombers out of ammo, sir.'

'Water cannon out of fuel, too, sir,' added Ricky.

Two men with expensive overcoats and wearing dark glasses, had left the car and were now standing behind the bulldozers. Jossy turned to Albert. 'I am starting to think that discretion may now be the better part of valour, old son. How about a tactical withdrawal – swift but dignified, eh?'

Before Albert could open his mouth, a new noise echoed above the revving of the bulldozers. A high-pitched squealing rang out to the left of the Giants' position. Everyone turned to look. A herd of twenty pigs of various shapes and sizes came stampeding into No-Man's Land between the wall and the bulldozers. Tracey was urging on the stampede with one-hand and holding a piece of paper in the other. 'Stop! Stop!' Tracey came to a halt below Jossy as the pigs milled around the bulldozers. The two men from the flash car looked worried for their posh coats.

Tracey addressed Jossy in a loud voice, like a victorious Roman General addressing Caesar. 'I have here an official letter stating that as from today a Preservation Order is placed on the whole area of St James' Park, formerly Canalside Stadium; the area to be all that is within two hundred yards of Moreton's Oak over there.'

'So it is Moreton's Oak after all,' muttered Harvey.

'Undoubtedly – yes!' Tracey whooped.

The drivers of the bulldozers and their bosses came close enough to hear.

'After the Civil War battle of Glipton, General Humphrey Moreton, badly wounded, hid in the branches of our oak tree. Then he was spirited away and nursed back to health by the local swineherds. He was so grateful that he granted free swine-grazing rights forever to the villagers of Glipton. Those rights still apply today. My researches prove that conclusively. The area is all the land within a two hundred-yard-radius of the oak tree.'

Jossy beamed and looked meaningfully at the bulldozer mafia. 'So that means nobody can lay a finger on our pitch.'

It said a lot for Tracey's confident explanation that the 'enemy' did not even ask to see the letter. They simply withdrew. Meanwhile, the Giants were having a great time pig chasing. A baby pig raced past Jossy, who scooped it up into his arms. Once again he mounted the barricade. 'Friends, Giants, countrymen, lend me your ears . . .'

'Mine are dirty but you can have 'em' offered Harvey.

Jossy ignored him. 'Who'd have thought that a bunch of animals would have been our salvation! Thanks to Tracey, assisted by Harvey and our good friend Councillor Fletcher, the Giants will live on here at St James' Park. It does my heart proud also to know that from this day forth, on this emerald turf, swine may safely graze.

Some of the applause was gently mocking.

'After Shakespeare, that speech, if I'm not mistaken,' said Ross.

'Yes – a long way after,' said Tracey.

Tracey suddenly climbed to the top of the barricade. 'Before all you weary warriors go home for your dinner, I am inviting you to a world première at the ice rink on Monday night. You all owe me a favour after today. Tickets will be available free at Jossy's shop. So I expect a hundred per cent turn out.'

'What's she up to?' asked Jossy.

'Oh she's probably got herself made Queen in the ice gala,' said Ross.

'Nothing would surprise me about that lassie,' said Jossy, in a voice of pure admiration.

The Giants filled one section of the front row of Glipton ice rink as the auditions for the Christmas Ice Show slid on. The 'Bolero' music began softly and slowly started to swell. The lights dimmed and a spotlight picked out two figures on the ice, poised ready to dance. It was Harvey and Tracey.

'It'll be a farce,' said Ross. 'He can't turn.'

Half of the Giants buried their faces in their hands as Tracey and Harvey swished to the end of the rink. As they approached the barrier, Tracey leaned into the turn and took Harvey round with her. It was not very graceful but at least Harvey stayed vertical. The Giants applauded. Glenn threw a set of plastic flowers.

Ricky whispered in Jossy's ear. 'There's a horse called Cool Porky running at Wincanton tomorrow. Want to chance it?'

Jossy glared at him. 'We can't have both of us working on instinct and coincidence. Forget it!'

NINE

A couple of days after the siege, Jossy was in extremely high spirits. Business at his shop was booming. Half the kids in Glipton and numbers of parents had taken up jogging. The Giants had just had a great training session with everybody giving their best. This was important, with the match against the Darnley Detonators coming up shortly to decide who would win the league.

Some of the lads had joined Jossy at the shop after training and now they were helping him 'decorate'. This consisted of plastering the walls with pictures of the Newcastle United greats. Jackie Milburn raced for goal; big Frank Brennan contested a header; Malcolm McDonald let fly with a special. Jossy stood back with a smile and almost a tear.

'Lovely, aren't they?'

'Did you know them?' asked Ricky.

'Pals, kidda. Pals, each one. I remember seeing Wor Jackie at Wembley. He nearly set the turf on fire.' Jossy was ablaze with nostalgia. 'One of these days I'm going to take you lot up there – on like a pilgrimage.'

'You've been saying that for ages. It'll never happen,' said Harvey.

'You never know your luck, kidda. Maybe in a year's time, with a few raffles and a donkey derby, the club funds will stretch to a visit to the real St James' Park. There'll be thunderclouds over the Leazes end, there'll be a touch of snow in the wind and a couple of seagulls blown up the river from Tynemouth . . .'

The phone in the back room rang. Glenn was nearest. He picked up the receiver and listened for a few seconds.

'I'll just get him.' Glenn looked as though he'd seen a ghost. He walked like a zombie towards Jossy.

'It's Bobby . . . Bobby Charlton on the phone for you.'

'Geddaway!' Jossy suddenly went white. He went into the back room, closing the door behind him.

'It's not a hoax, is it?' asked Ross.

Glenn shook his head and they waited with bated breath.

Five minutes later Jossy came out, chuffed as anything. Albert came into the shop as the torrent started. 'Bobby Charlton, personally, on the phone to me . . .'

'Wants your advice on buying a player, eh?' joked Albert.

'Better than that, honest! He wants me to go up for a testimonial match against the old enemy, Sunderland. Imagine, me running out there again at St James'. That's in three months' time. But better than that, he wants us *all* to go – and he'll show us round. How about that? Talk about dreams coming true.'

'Sorry to sound like a wet blanket, Jossy, but we're skint.' Albert's words brought disappointed looks from the lads. Jossy pulled another poster from under the counter. He unrolled it to reveal Bobby Charlton in Manchester United colours.

'Come on – give me a hand to put it up.'

'But he never played for Newcastle,' said Harvey.

'He's still one of the lads,' insisted Jossy.

They had just about finished putting up the poster when Councillor Glenda Fletcher flounced into the shop. There was a look of proper pride on her face that obviously related to her efforts to help them save St James' Park. Jossy smoothed back a lick of hair and spoke as posh and polite as he could.

'Oh good evening, Councillor Fletcher. Joining the jogging set? Or is this just a social call?'

Glenda looked round the shop to make sure that she had an audience. She gave a special conspiratorial look to Tracey.

'I just wanted to say how delighted I was to be of some assistance in saving your ground. And may I say a special word about Miss Gaunt's efforts. Practical, methodical – a credit to our sex.'

The boys sensed that Glenda was pushing things. She continued: 'I gather that you men were larking about in some kind of charade – playing soldiers I'm told – whilst Tracey burrowed away . . .'

Jossy flushed at this and broke in: 'Protest can take many forms, Councillor. I'll not have my lads' efforts run down. It was not a charade, it was a siege.'

'Boys will be boys,' said Glenda acidly.

The atmosphere was now thick with tension. Glenda twisted the knife.

'Mr Blair. I think you do wonders for our local community here in Glipton. You have boundless enthusiasm, lovely ideas . . .' the Giants waited for the putdown . . . 'but I'm afraid when it comes to organisation you're stumped. That's when we girls have to be called in.'

The boys looked at Jossy, whose face was now beetroot red. 'I call in who I like, when I like. Now, we're busy here, Councillor. *Organising* my shop.' Jossy was about to turn his back on Glenda when Tracey chipped in.

'You've got to admit that women tend to be more practical, Jossy. You're a rotten organiser.'

That did it. Jossy rounded on them. 'Typical! Put two women together and they'll form a committee. Within a week they'll be running your life and your business; in a fortnight the world.'

'Hear, hear!' shouted Harvey.

The shop was now a battlefield. Glenda seized the moment. 'Why don't we decide who's best by a sporting contest? I propose that Tracey and I get a netball team together and give you, er, men, a game.'

Jossy looked at the lads.

'We'll murder them,' hissed Ross.

The other Giants growled their agreement. Without another word, Tracey and Glenda left the shop. Jossy turned to the lads.

'OK. I want you all down the Community Centre tomorrow night at six. We'll have a practice and I'll pick the team. A bit of daft netball will be good training for the league decider against the Dets.'

'We'll murder those women,' said Harvey.

'Doddle,' said Ross.

By six-thirty the next night Jossy had whittled down his netball squad to seven. They were himself, Harvey, Glenn, Selly, Ross, Ricky and Wayne Chapman. In fact the boys were the cream of the Giants but so far they had shown more enthusiasm than skill at throwing a ball around accurately. Things were not helped either by Jossy's belief that netball and basketball were the same game. A couple of the lads had pointed out the difference to him, but he swanned along blithely.

'Come on lads, form a circle.' As the boys did, Jossy produced a cassette player from his hold-all and switched it on. The strains of 'Sweet Georgia Brown' filled the gym. Jossy stood in the middle of the circle and began hand dribbling the ball.

'OK, you lot, start jogging right to left. The world's greatest netballers are the Harlem Globetrotters. They practise to music. Change direction when I shout.'

Pretty soon the 'practice' had degenerated into crafty

hand dribbling and fancy shooting at the net. When they packed up an hour later Jossy had not even sorted out who was going to play where.

On the day of the game half of Glipton Secondary School had turned out in the schoolyard to watch the netball match. Glenda's team were warming up at one end and most impressive they looked. Glenda had not told anyone that she had been a very good player and was still a selector for the county junior sides. So the five girls she had chosen to join herself and Tracey were no mugs. The goal shooter was a big, strapping girl who had the accuracy of a heat-seeking missile on the net. And some of Tracey's passing during the warm-up was spot on.

The battered old Toyota van that the Giants knocked about in swept into the yard with Albert driving. Daz and Dean raised a pathetic chant of 'Giants, Giants' as Jossy led a motley crew out of the back of the van. The team were all wearing Giants' football strips above the waist but below the waist some of them seemed more suited for an ice hockey match. Glenn and Selly each wore shinguards. They had heard that girls could play pretty rough at netball. Harvey was very worried about his legs and his future in ice skating; he had even thought about taking out insurance. So he was wearing tracksuit trousers that appeared to be full of foam rubber. He was in fact wearing cricket thigh pads and thick knee bandages. It was obvious that mobility about the pitch was not going to be a strong factor in the Giant's play.

Miss Lanchester, the school History teacher, was to be the referee. She was a small young woman, fit-looking, and very soft spoken. After the teams had warmed up for five minutes, she called up the captains.

'I know that there's an element of grudge in this

101

match, so I shall be very firm. Any rough play or verbal violence will be severely dealt with.'

Jossy looked wrily at Glenda and offered to shake hands. Glenda merely glared at him, then jogged back to her position as goal defence. Jossy noticed the positions the girls had taken up. He turned to the lads and gave them a brief tactics talk.

'Harvey. Defend that net! I'll play up front. The rest of you, spread out!'

Tracey heard this and began to laugh. This enraged Jossy. At the whistle he began back pedalling with the ball, screaming at Ross to get up front. The whistle shrieked. Miss Lanchester walked over.

'No stepping. No holding the ball.'

Jossy's mouth fell open. Tracey took the ball from him with a wink.

'Different ball game I'm afraid, Boss!'

Tracey passed the ball high and hard to the strapping shooter. Harvey leapt about like a nervous sack racer. The girl popped the ball into the net. The floodgates had opened. Jossy did not even get time to hand dribble. By half-time the score was 15–0 to the girls and the Giants were bushed and almost unable to suck their oranges. Ross flopped down next to Jossy.

'I told you we were practising the wrong game. Even the Harlem Globetrotters would have bother handling this lot.'

It was not in Jossy's nature to even think of defeat. He looked across at the girls, who had not even needed to rest their legs. 'It's certainly a lot tougher than I thought it was going to be. I think we ought to play it a bit more physical in the second half.'

This theory proved to be the complete undoing of the Giants. From the start of the second half Jossy prowled the pitch like a scalp-crazy Apache. He leaned on Tracey, then took up a position under the net by

Glenda and began yelling at the top of his voice.

'Come on lads! Jockey them, jockey them.' Jossy pranced up and down, ignoring the amused look on Glenda's face. At last the ball flew towards the girls' net. Glenda jumped to take it and Jossy crowded her, flapping his arms. Jossy tried to knock it out of her hands. The ball trickled away and Glenda fell to the ground clutching her fingers.

'I never touched her,' insisted Jossy, as Miss Lanchester arrived, whistling like mad. Glenda writhed on the ground. 'What an actress!' complained Jossy.

'Off!' Miss Lanchester pointed to the touch-line.

'What for?' asked Jossy, 'Unladylike conduct?'

Miss Lanchester ignored the jibe and Jossy left the action. When the final whistle went, the score was 33–0 to the ladies, though most people had stopped counting and more than half the crowd had gone home. Jossy's bedraggled team limped off and flopped by the van. Albert and Bob Nelson were lost for words. Councillor Glenda Fletcher was not. She strode towards them like Boadicea on the rampage.

'She's going to gloat again,' said Ross.

Jossy stood up and tried to muster a little dignity. Most of the non-netballing Giants had gathered. Tracey looked pleased, but she was not full of herself like Glenda was.

'Right, then.' Glenda addressed her remarks to Jossy. 'Do you now dispute that we women are as good as men – given an equal game?'

'You win Councillor. But aren't you rubbing it in a bit?'

'Far from it.' Glenda looked round at her audience. Even Bob Nelson was paying maximum attention, trying to work out what she was after. She put it fairly bluntly. 'I think recent events suggest that I'd be an ideal person to have on the Glipton Giants' committee.'

A buzz ran around the gathering. Most of the boys shook their heads. But Bob, Albert and Jossy looked impressed. Tracey quietly began to seethe. Her intuition told her that Glenda was hungry for power.

Glenda played a trump card. 'As you all probably know, I am Chairwoman of the Sports and Leisure Committee of the council. In that capacity I control a fund to promote sporting activities. I gather that you have been offered a team visit to Newcastle United's ground.' She looked round to see the impact her words were having. It was effective. 'If I am elected to your committee, I will see that the money is available for you, Jossy, to take the boys to Tyneside.'

Jossy's face showed that he had swallowed the bait. The boys did not need any more persuading. Tracey was jumping with rage. She started to speak but Jossy stopped her.

'Of course, we'll have to have a vote, Councillor, but I think you can take it as definite that we are interested.'

'Interested?' Bob hissed in Jossy's ear. 'Snap the offer up! Make her Life President!'

'I suggest you have a vote – soon.' Knowing the value of suspense, Glenda made her exit.

'Tyneside, here we come,' said Harvey.

The lads began drifting off. Tracey dragged Jossy to one side. She was almost in tears.

'It's a bribe Jossy – a rotten bribe. That woman is power mad.'

Jossy was amazed. 'Ten minutes ago you were her pal, all girls together. Women of Glipton unite and put the fellas' in their place!'

Tracey sagged and spoke quietly. 'She's like Cleopatra with Mark Antony. She's a snake in sheep's clothing.'

Jossy grinned and spoke in a croaky voice, caused by too much yelling during the netball match. 'You're a bright, honest lassie but I think you're way off beam about Glenda. She's going to get us to Newcastle.'

'Yes,' sighed Tracey, 'but even dreams can have too high a price.'

The run-up to the vital match against the Dets was a disaster for Jossy. He had developed a bad chest cold as a result of the netball match. At the meeting to vote on Glenda's joining the committee, his voice went altogether. Not that it mattered. Glenda was voted in unanimously, with Tracey walking out just before the votes were cast. Most of the Giants put this down to Tracey being jealous of another powerful female joining the club. They all reckoned she would be back soon.

On the day before the Dets match Jossy was forced to retire to his bed. He lay, pale and pathetic, surrounded by the Giants and his room was swamped in grapes, flowers and Lucozade. His face was deathly white and he could not speak a word. By the side of the bed was a note-pad and pencil. Albert was doing his best to outline tactics for the big game.

'I think that Jossy will agree that we take the measure of the Dets in the first twenty minutes. So it's up to you, Ricky, to keep the defence tight.'

Jossy scribbled on his pad and held it up. The message read, 'Correct. Give no quarter'. The tactics talk went on in this vein for a good half-hour and then the lads took their leave.

Jossy's last scribbled message was to Albert alone. 'Do it for me, son.'

Albert grinned and pinched a handful of Jossy's grapes. He paused as he got to the door. There was a worried look on his face.

'Councillor Fletcher sent her best regards. She says you haven't to worry a bit. The team are in good hands.'

Jossy winked and lay back, day-dreaming of a resounding victory.

TEN

Bob and Albert watched with keen interest as the Darnley Detonators played shooty-in at the oak tree end of St James' Park. There was no doubting it – they looked good. They had an easy confidence about their shooting and passing that spoke volumes. There were lads in the team from as far away as Huddersfield and Bolton – it was going to be a tough match for the Giants. As Selly kicked off, Bob tried to ease the tension.

'Far be it from me to wish Jossy any harm, but isn't it nice to think that we're in for ninety minutes of football without all that shouting and bawling?'

Albert nodded. 'He'll be leaping around that bed like a lop.'

Neither of them noticed a bicycle pull up on the opposite side of the pitch and a tracksuited figure wearing a baseball cap stalk up to the touch-line brandishing a loud hailer. But the familiar voice shook up the Giants and their supporters.

'On your toes, Giants. On your toes. I won't have any slacking. I want maximum effort. Ross, go and find that ball.' Glenda normally sounded bossy but, thanks to the loud hailer, she sounded like Darth Vader. The effect on the Giants was disastrous. Ross charged upfield for a ball that he had no chance of getting. Ricky yelled at him to get back and mark his opposing winger. The Dets exploited the gap and scored a simple goal.

Albert and Bob raced up to the self-appointed coach.

'What are you trying to do, woman – apart form make us a laughing stock?' Bob's moustache bristled.

'You're putting the lads off,' yelled Albert. 'Your screaming at Ross just then cost us a goal.'

Glenda looked at them as though they had just crawled out from under a stone. 'I fear that you gentlemen are forgetting that I am an *elected* member of the Glipton Giants' Committee. What authority do you two claim?'

'I founded this club,' said Albert pointedly.

'They were the Grasshoppers then, Mr Hanson. That was the *past*.'

Bob looked at Albert. There was very little they could do short of grievous bodily harm, so they mooched back to the other side of the pitch.

'We can hardly start yelling at the lads to take no notice of her. That'll just doubly confuse them,' said Bob bitterly. 'I'm going to sit in the car.'

Bob stormed off. Albert watched morosely as the Dets patiently built up yet another attack. Harvey ran out to collect an awkward bouncing ball. He was about to time his jump for it when Glenda's voice pierced the air. 'You should have been out quicker, McGinn. Alert, boy, alert!' Harvey half turned to look in her direction and slipped. The ball bobbled over the line and into the net. Albert withdrew to the back of the stand, while on the pitch the Giants began to squabble amongst themselves. They were lucky to be only two down when the whistle went for half-time.

The Giants flopped down in a huddle while Ricky walked round them trying to lift morale.

'Come on, lads, heads up. Let's do it for Jossy.'

'Why should we?' They all turned to Ross. 'Jossy wanted that woman on the committee. Now she thinks she's boss of the world.'

'We *all* voted.' Ricky was disillusioned too. 'What can we do? If we tell her to push off she'll not support the trip to Newcastle.'

Harvey had his brightest idea for a long time. 'Dumb insolence. That's the answer. I once got put into detention for that. Just ignore her.'

Nobody disagreed. When Glenda approached them they acted as though she wasn't there.

'This is a disgraceful team performance.' Glenda waited for a reply. None came. 'Oh, I see. You've given up! Wait until I tell Mr Blair.'

Ricky broke the silence. 'We'll talk to you in the dressing-room after the match – Councillor.'

Glenda turned and nodded stiffly. Ricky winked at the lads.

In the second half, despite silence from Glenda and a better display from the Giants, the Dets held on to their two-goal advantage. It gave them the league title. As the crowd dispersed, Ricky led the Giants quiety into the dressing-room. Once inside he spoke: 'Today I've had enough of Councillor Fletcher. I don't care what she does – she can cancel our Newcastle trip if she wants – but I say we teach her a lesson.'

There were roars of approval.

'Get changed fast, then.'

Five minutes later Glenda tapped on the door.

'Come in Councillor,' shouted Harvey, his voice full of politeness. No sooner had Glenda opened the door than she was bundled into a corner and the Giants raced out. Ricky looked like a cat who had got the cream as he locked the door. Inside Glenda was calling them some names that she usually reserved for the opposition party on the council.

The band of highly-amused Giants ran past Tracey Gaunt who had watched the proceedings on and off the field from behind the oak tree. Ricky and Ross stopped on the steps of the changing room. Tracey looked at the key that Ricky was holding in triumph.

'Councillor Fletcher has been put in her place, I guess,' Tracey laughed.

'Not before time. You were dead right about her,' said Ross.

'I'll take that.' Tracey pointed at the key. 'You never know. I might be walking past here in an hour or two's time and just happen to hear a voice crying in the wilderness.'

'Through a loud hailer,' added Ross.

Jossy was having the kind of dream that all football managers like to have. The Giants were parading the F.A. Cup around Wembley Stadium. The fans were going wild. Somebody stuck a daft black-and-white striped hat on Jossy's head. A television reporter grabbed him and asked him to explain his marvellous tactics. 'Better watch I don't speak too broad . . .' he was thinking.

Reality burst into his bedroom in the form of Bob and Albert. 'Did you tell that woman she could shout at the team just because she's on the committee?' Bob, as usual, was eager to believe the worst of people.

Jossy tried to collect his wits.

'Did we win?' he scribbled on his pad.

'Did we win!' Bob was fuming. 'Your mate the Councillor made sure we didn't! You'd have thought she was skipper of the *Ark Royal*. Cap, loud hailer, screaming like a banshee. Did you say she could coach the team in your absence?'

'NO!' Jossy's pen nearly went through the pad.

It took half the writing pad to convince Bob that Jossy had in no way delegated power to Glenda. Then Bob and Albert went home muttering awful things about loud-mouthed females.

Jossy had half expected the lads to drop in but when seven o'clock came and went he reckoned that the disappointment was something they did not want to share for a while.

A tap came to his bedroom door and he prepared himself to meet visitors. Tracey popped around the door. Jossy beamed. Five minutes later he was laughing all over his face as Tracey outlined the come-uppance the boys had dished out to Glenda. Then Tracey described a little plan of her own; one last bit of revenge.

The night before the Giants' trip to Tyneside saw particularly hectic activity in two households in Glipton.

Councillor Glenda Fletcher had spent the six days since the Dets match calming ruffled feathers. She had talked to Tracey, forgiven the boys their prank and grovelled to Jossy. Now she had just finished packing a small suitcase.

At Tracey Gaunt's house Tracey was packing too. It surprised her parents. And Tracey had a bigger surprise in store for her father.

'Dad, I want you to make a phone call for me. It's a bit of a con but it's all in a good cause.'

Fortunately her father knew Councillor Glenda Fletcher so he agreed, after a five-minute explanation by his daughter, to help put the lady in her place.

The phone rang in Glenda's house and Glenda answered.

'Councillor Glenda Fletcher here . . .'

Within two minutes she was buying a line that really flattered her. 'On the shortlist for the sports council in this area! My, this is so sudden. An interview in London tomorrow afternoon? Well, I had other plans, but they can be altered. Yes, I'll be there at 3 o'clock.'

The polite male voice on the other end thanked her profusely. Tracey's dad put down the phone. He nodded t the suitcase. 'No prizes for guessing who takes the Councillor's place on the coach to Geordie-land!'

Tracey gave him a hug.

n the night, Tracey realised what harm it would do to he team if the Councillor actually made the trip to London. So she slipped a polite note of apology into Councillor Fletcher's little house before she joined the Giants' coach. Spirits were riding high as the coach approached the Tyne Bridge. Tracey sat in the front eat next to Jossy who was doing the full tourist guide it. It was obvious that the visit to the real St James' Park had him jangling with excitement.

'Observe, good people, the glorious city of Newcastle. Land of leeks, stotty cake and the finest football team in he world.'

There were cries of 'rubbish'.

'To your right the river winds away to the shipyards where the lads build the biggest ships in the world. To our left, a couple of miles upstream, and you're in some of the finest scenery in England.'

Harvey was not going to let this praise go unchallenged. 'I read that the Tyne is one of the most polluted rivers in England. All the fish are dead.'

'I'll walk on the water and find out,' said Jossy.

They were now in the shadow of the floodlight pylons of St James' Park and a totally different mood had overcome Jossy. The kids sensed this, and the banter died away as the coach stopped.

Jossy stepped off like a pilgrim visiting Mecca. He looked up at the giant stands. His knees felt wobbly and there was a tight feeling in his chest. If only . . . he pushed the nostalgia from his mind.

Bobby Charlton's greeting was powerful and friendly. He greeted Jossy like an old mate. Ross just could not resist the question that they all wanted answering.

'Just how good was Jossy, Mr Charlton? Did you ever see him play?'

There was no hesitation. 'He was a great player. If he hadn't been injured he'd have become a legend here and an England player for sure.' Jossy blushed.

The Giants told Bobby about their defeat by the Dets in the league decider and of the coming Cup Final. Bobby launched into a pep talk. 'Forget tactics in the Cup, just play your guts out. When we were winning at Manchester we used to attack like crazy in the Cup.'

During this Jossy nodded constant agreement, though Harvey for one would have taken bets that Jossy's theories would be different before the big match.

'Could we go out on the pitch?' asked Ricky in a hushed voice.

'Certainly,' said Bobby.

The Giants ran out kicking a ball and Tracey watched as Jossy jogged after them. Suddenly he stopped and looked up into the empty terraces. It was not hard to imagine them filled with thousands of the Geordie faithful. Harvey had taken up position in goal. Jossy called for the ball, trapped it and began a headlong dribble past the Giants. He let fly at goal from twenty yards out and the net bulged. Again Jossy raised his head to the terraces. He wiped away a tear. One or two of the lads began to sing 'Blaydon Races'. Jossy joined in.

At five o'clock the next afternoon the coach was whizzing through the market town of Thirsk when Jossy screamed to the driver to stop.

'It's a bit early for fish and chips, Jossy,' said Tracey.

They all stared out of the coach windows as Jossy ran into a newsagent's shop and came out with an evening paper. He buried his head in it, then climbed back on the coach and glowered at Ricky.

'Tyneside Tessie. Sure thing in the first race at Haydock. Fell at the third fence. Brill.'

Ricky shrugged. 'With all the good luck of the past few days, Boss, you've got to expect a few minor setbacks.'

Jossy led them into 'On Top of Old Smokey' for the third time. It was one of the few songs to which he knew all the words.

ELEVEN

One of the basic troubles with Jossy Blair was that he never knew when he was on to a really good thing. Like most dreamers, he liked to take chances – and sometimes he took one too many.

A couple of days after the trip to Newcastle, Jossy was arranging the display in his shop window. Business was going really well and all that was on his mind was the Cup Final against the Dets on the coming Saturday. The two 'gentlemen' who walked through his door soon turned his mind to other matters. Both were built like Rugby League players; both had faces that had been 're-arranged' at various times; both were obviously heavies. Jossy had a pretty good idea why they were calling on him.

'Lanergan's lads are you?' Jossy was trying the brazen touch. 'Which zoo did he find you two in?'

'Oh, a patter merchant,' said the heavy with blond hair and a tattoo on his throat. 'It makes the finale of our business so much more fun when we get a cheeky one.'

The other heavy, meanwhile, was casting his eyes around Jossy's stock.

'There'll be no need to re-possess or do the joint over,' said Jossy pointedly. 'Tell Mr Lanergan that I'll have the money on the counter of his betting shop in a week. £200 exactly.'

Jossy had no idea how he could raise the money; he was just trying to buy time. He knew that he had been a mug to get involved with two bookies.

The heavy looking over Jossy's gear picked up a box of trainers. He took one out and slowly tore the sole off. 'If we don't get money, we'll remove goods to the appropriate value, Mr Blair.'

His blond colleague came up close to Jossy. 'So just get the money soon, eh? And don't try running away; we'll be keeping tabs on you.'

They both left the shop. The grin vanished from Jossy's face; he was running a bit short of good fairies.

Ten minutes later Bob Nelson breezed into the shop. 'Hello Jossy. What's the matter? You look as though you've lost a fiver and found a twenty-pence piece.'

'I can't be laughing boy all the time, Bob,' Jossy tried to be cheerful but it was tough going.

'I've got a wheeze that will cheer you up.' Bob was buzzing with enthusiasm. 'Thanks largely to you, this has been a great season for our lads. It would be wonderful to mark it with a disco on Saturday night after the Cup Final. I've checked out the Community Centre and we can have it free. We can have a trophy or two for the best players. We can have a buffet – and I'll provide the disco music and be the DJ myself.'

As usual money was one of the first things to cross Jossy's mind. 'Club funds aren't too good, Bob.'

'Forget that.' A somewhat crafty look had come into Bob's eye. 'I can provide what I've just outlined for – let's say – three quid a ticket, payable at the door.'

Jossy looked at him hard.

'OK.' Bob was wriggling. 'I don't do it at a loss – but I'm certainly not out to make a profit.'

'Of course not,' Jossy laughed. 'It's a grand idea. I'll spell you on the DJ bit.'

Bob Nelson's enthusiasm was really on the boil. Th
next evening when Jossy showed up at St James' Park
the white Mercedes was parked at the back of th
grandstand and Bob's throaty Yorkshire tones could l
heard urging on the lads in sprint training. Jossy did n
mind this but usually there were motives in Bob's min
that were not always obvious.

'I want you to run for every ball on Saturday. You'
faster than the Dets. Let's see you run them ragged
Bob roared.

'Got a bet on the lads for the final, then?' asked Joss
as he came up behind Bob.

Bob turned round as though he had been shot. H
looked guilty. 'Only a small one. With a pal from th
golf club. Adds a bit of extra interest.' Jossy chose to sa
nothing. He toyed with the idea of a bet on the Giants t
solve his money problem, but kicked it into touch.
was unlucky to bet on your team.

Jossy rapidly put his problem out of his mind. He ha
had a brainwave that would liven up the trainin
session and give the lads a real workout. He called th
squad to gather round.

'Now then my bonny lads. We've had the inspiratio
of a visit to the promised land to get us ready for the Cu
Final. Now I've got an old Geordie game to put sprin
in your limbs and iron in your muscles.'

'Is this football or the Mr Universe competition
asked Harvey.

Jossy did not bother to answer.

'The game is called Mount A Cuddy and it require
two teams. So, Ricky lead one and Ross the other.
shall demonstrate the cuddy with Ricky's team.

Jossy walked over to the goalpost and leaned his bac
on it. 'I am the buffer. Now, Ricky and the lads, form
row of backs in front of me.'

Ricky's team did so, each locking arms firmly aroun

the knees of the person in front.

'Now. One at a time, Ross, get your team to jump on.'

'Jump on! You'll have us all crippled,' yelled Harvey from the middle of the cuddy.

'Hold fast,' replied Jossy, 'You have three jumps each, unless the cuddy breaks.'

The boys hurled themselves into the game with gusto. The odd shin got barked, and the cuddy buckled several times, but soon Jossy took a breather and let the lads get on with it. He laughed heartily each time the buffer men had to take the jolt of a man landing.

Suddenly Jossy's attention was drawn to two figures lurking by the wooden stile that led from their field to the canal bank. It was Lanergan's boys. The blond one beckoned Jossy over. Making sure the Giants were engrossed in the game, Jossy jogged across the pitch to the stile.

'I think it's great the patience and effort you put in with those little lads, Mr Blair.' The blond heavy was filing his nails. 'I'm afraid we've got some bad news for you – and your lads. Our boss is involved with a sizeable wager concerning your game with the Dets on Saturday. And he requires that your team *lose*. If they *win*, then we will make sure that you pay the penalty – if you'll excuse the football reference.'

The other heavy chuckled.

'I will not throw a football match. You and your boss can do what you like to me or my shop. No chance.' Jossy was trembling with anger.

'Suit yourself. If your side loses, our boss says maybe you can have more time to come up with the two hundred oncers.'

Jossy wasted no more time listening. 'No chance,' he rapped, as he jogged away back to the training session.

The day of the final dawned crisp, bright and optimistic

for everybody connected with the Giants – except Jossy. He sat in the back room of his shop with a mug of tea and tried to fight back the ocean of self-pity and regret that was threatening to drown him.

He looked round at what weeks of hard work and inspiration from the Glipton Giants had brought him. Newcastle United had been good to him after his injury. The money for the shop had come from the money they had paid him in 1971 and the interest it had gathered in the bank. He walked to the blackboard and looked fondly at all the arrows outlining tactics. All the good memories of games won, games lost – but most of all, experiences shared – flooded back. 'Come on, son,' he murmured to himself, 'get a grip. If you're going to go down, go down with flying colours.'

Tracey caught him just before the mood of defeat vanished. She slipped into the shop with an enormous black-and-white rosette that she had made specially for the Cup Final.

'You look as though you're ill, Jossy.' Tracey looked hard at him.

'Worry. Tension. When you're a manager you live on your nerves, love.'

The battered white Toyota van whizzed along the main road through the suburbs. Out of the windows fluttered black-and-white scarves and Albert crouched over the wheel with Jossy by his side. All at once a clattering started from the engine and within seconds the van had ground to a halt.

'Great,' said Jossy. 'Cup Final day and here's us stuck on the hard shoulder.'

Albert had several goes at starting the engine but they were all in vain. Then Jossy had a brainwave. 'All out,' he shouted to the vanful of Giants, 'we'll get the bus.'

Five minutes later the team were wedged in between some not-very-pleased lady shoppers on the top deck of a bus stuck in heavy traffic in the centre of Manchester. Jossy looked at his watch, saw that they had only forty minutes to kick off and order emergency action.

'Right you lot. Start getting changed.'

'We'll get chucked off!' yelled Ricky.

'Not with my line in chat,' said Jossy. He went down to the front of the bus and gave an impromptu speech to the shoppers. 'Ladies, I am Jossy Blair, manager of the Glipton Giants. We are on our way to a vital match. We apologise for any inconvenience we might cause by getting changed on this bus but it's our only hope. Any of you of a nervous disposition should avert your eyes, though all reasonable attempts at modesty will be made. Thank you.'

It worked. There were one or two grumbles but no aggro until the conductor appeared on the scene.

Jossy had just pulled out the tactics board and was deeply engrossed. 'From the back. Harvey, I want you to be a rock. Chuck the ball out firmly to Ricky.'

The conductor had a host of Manchester United badges on his cap and his shirt. He peered over Jossy's shoulder at the plastic men spread around the board. At first Jossy did not notice him.

'Ricky, you must provide plenty of ball for our twin strikers and Ross.' Jossy moved the three plastic men upfield.

'You're never playing three men up front, are you pal?' The conductor obviously had very strong views on the finer points of the game. 'One's all you need provided the mid-field can pass. Here!'

He grabbed the two blue plastic men that represented Glenn and Selly and moved them back to mid-field. Jossy moved them back. The conductor's hand went to pick them up again. Jossy restrained it. For a second they arm wrestled. A hush fell over the bus.

'I am the manager of this team,' said Jossy firmly. 'You conduct your bus and I'll give the team talk.'

'Not on my bus you won't,' replied the conductor. 'I want you off this bus. Now!' The conductor pointed up the aisle with his free hand.

'Don't be daft,' said Jossy. 'I've got to get to the match with my team.'

'If you don't get off now, I'll get a copper to put you off. Right!'

Jossy realised that pleading would be no use. He accepted the situation.

'Do your best lads. I'll see you as soon as I can.'

He sloped off down the aisle with what grace he could muster. A pathetic wave was all he could manage as the bus swept on.

There was nobody else at the bus-stop. A wave of self-pity welled up and Jossy kicked the waste-bin at the base of a lamp-post. It hurt his foot. The Giants poised for greatness! The biggest day in the club's history! And where's the Manager? Swanning about Manchester needing a lift and worried sick about his gambling debts. Jossy spared himself no grim detail in his thoughts.

A young lass carrying a bunch of bright shopping bags formed a queue behind him. 'When's the next 42 pet?' asked Jossy.

'Half an hour. Though they sometimes miss.' The girl turned her attention back to her chewing gum.

Panic began setting in. A clock in an insurance office across the street said five to three. The lads would be sweating . . . Tracey would be doing her nut . . . Albert would be pacing . . . Bob would be on the verge of bad language . . . The Dets would be laughing . . .

The Hell's Angel did not normally stop for hitch-hikers,

but this one looked a case. The ape-hanger handlebars drew level with Jossy, who was now slumped on the hard-shoulder, having sprinted two miles only to find himself high above the centre of the city on the Mancunian Way fly-over. Jossy's tracksuit was sticking to him and his face was red. The only energetic bit of his whole body was the flagging thumb.

'Jump on, pal.' The hairy face and the greasy leathers did not put Jossy off. He dragged himself up behind the Angel. The engine roared and off they whizzed.

'I want to go to Wennington Green Football Ground – please,' Jossy shouted above the slipstream.

The Angel did not seem very interested. He had already assumed that Jossy was a fellow raver, footloose and fancy-free on the highway. 'On the run are you, pal?' Giving the Law a run for its money?'

'No. I'm a Football Manager. My team's in the Cup Final this afternoon. Do me a favour.' Jossy tried, but half the words got lost on the wind.

'Football Manager! You're a card. They all knock about in Rollers with cigars and mohair suits.' The Angel looked round.

'Look. I'll buy you a drink when we've burned up the tarmac to Coventry – and you can tell me the real story.'

'Coventry!' Jossy began to plead again as the speedometer nudged towards the ton. It took another twenty miles before Jossy got the message through and they turned round.

Bob Nelson's language was not very gentlemanly when he saw Jossy legging it up to the touch-line at the Cup Final. Jossy paid very little attention to Bob's attack. He sought out Tracey and was surprised to find her in tears.

'What's the damage, kid?'

Tracey looked at him in a way that demanded a full

explanation. 'Three nil,' she said in a flat voice.

'Look,' said Jossy, 'I hitched a lift with a Hell's Angel and he took me for a ride.'

'The lads think you got side-tracked. And Bob hasn't helped. He's been calling you everything. Why don't you find some way to explain things.'

Jossy saw the sense in what she said. The problem was how to get on the field. Ricky was looking across at Jossy. Tracey started back as Jossy began to do a crazy pantomime of someone who had swallowed poison. He hurled himself on the ground, legs kicking and clutching his stomach. Ricky got the message. Next tackle, he deliberately stumbled and rolled around the pitch in apparent agony. Jossy and Tracey, with her bucket and sponge, were beside him in a second.

'I'm sorry I couldn't make if for the kick-off, Rick, but I did try. I'll explain to everyone later. I know the lads are downhearted, but get stuck in. Remember what Bobby Charlton said. Guts and heart are more important than tactics in a Cup Final.'

'OK, Boss. Glad you made it after all.'

The Dets did not know what hit them. Ricky stormed through the middle like a train; Glenn and Selly moved the ball like lightning; Ross found his shooting boots. At full time the score stood at 3–3. The match would be decided by a penalty shoot-out.

Ricky won the toss and there was tense silence as the Dets' goalkeeper took his place in goal to face the first Giant. Ross stepped up and hit the ball hard. The goalie got a hand to it but the ball spun into the net. 1–0 to the Giants. The first Det missed. Next up for the Giants was Selly who mis-cued hopelessly as the ball ran wide of the post. The Det scored. 1–1. Wayne scored for the Giants. A Det made it 2–2. Glenn made it 3–2. The next Det scored. 3–3. Ricky blasted the ball home. 4–3. It was now all up to Harvey. The Det hit the ball a mighty whack. Harvey dived too early but the ball cannoned off his heels. The Giants had won the cup.

Jossy Blair danced with his lads as though there was no tomorrow – and no day of reckoning on Monday.

The Glipton Giants' disco was in full swing when Ross brought his father the takings from the door. Bob was still sweating from his stint as DJ. In his pocket were two hundred pounds from Lanergan, paid surprisingly quickly. 'Not bad, dad. Two hundred and three pounds at the door.'

Bob took the money, as a deputation, led by Tracey, approached. 'Can we see you in private for a little while please, Mr Nelson?'

Bob was in a wonderful mood. His own profit on the takings was £50 and it was always nice to get one over on Lanergan. 'Certainly. What is it? Plans for next season?'

Tracey nodded. 'Yes, like keeping our manager in reasonably good health.'

In the next ten minutes Bob heard the story of Jossy's cash problems and about Lanergan's strong-arm tactics to try and get Jossy to throw the game.

Maybe it was the dishing of Lanergan that persuaded Bob to make his gesture. . . .

The presentation of trophies was the last item on the bill. Tracey was appointed Mistress of Ceremonies, and she asked Jossy to step up and present the two awards. He read from a piece of paper: 'To the Player of the Year, this handsome trophy. The winner is – Ricky Sweet.' Ricky collected the trophy and the applause. Jossy read on: 'Club Personality of the Year – Bob Nelson!' Bob was genuinely surprised at this, but Tracey was not. She had lobbied very strongly in Bob's favour!

Jossy was in full swing: 'We've had a great season. I am proud to stand here and salute the Glipton Giants – a team fit to be mentioned in the same breath as the Mighty Magpies – Newcastle United.'

Then Tracey made her move. She stepped forward with a small parcel and addressed the crowd. 'As the last stage of our proceedings tonight we have a special award to our manager, Jossy Blair. We gather that he is being hounded –' Jossy looked alarmed – 'so we offer him a little solid help and advice.'

Jossy took the parcel gingerly and unwrapped it. Eyes popping, he unbelievingly started to count out the bank notes the parcel contained.

'Read the note, Jossy,' Tracey whispered in his ear.

Jossy read the message on top of the bank notes. 'Please use this £203 wisely – and stick to honest bookies. Signed – A friend.'

Jossy and Bob exchanged winks. As Jossy stepped down from the stage he peeled off three pound notes.

'Here Tracey. Put this in the bank as the start of our fund for the trip to München Gladbach.'

Tracey took the money.

'Albert. I want you to check out hotels, drinking water, training pitches . . .'

Harvey could not resist: 'Race tracks, betting shops! *Auf wiedersehen* another two hundred smackers – if we don't watch him!'

If you have enjoyed this book here are some more exciting BBC/Knight titles you may like to read:

SEAVIEW

CHRIS BARLAS

It all began when George and Sandy's dad was made redundant from the supermarket. With his golden handshake, he bought Seaview, a small private hotel in Blackpool.

George was very fond of Leeds: all his friends were here, his school, his favourite walks. Everything he knew about life he'd learned in Leeds. He didn't want to move. Not even to Blackpool. At 13, he didn't want to start life all over again.

Post·A·Book

Royal Mail service in association with the Book Marketing Council & The Booksellers Association.

Post-A-Book is a Post Office trademark.

BREAK POINT

JEREMY BURNHAM

Barry pushed past his trainer and opened the door – then turned back, shaking with fury. 'You said I was using tennis to get out from under,' he heard himself saying. 'Well, you was right. And if that gets up your nose, you can take a running jump. I'll make it on me own.'

Talent and determination alone won't make Barry a tennis champion. Can he succeed against all the odds?

BBC/KNIGHT BOOKS

A QUESTION OF SPORT

HAZEL LEWTHWAITE

Do you know:

which sport has laundry handed out at the end?
(Emlyn Hughes didn't)

where you'd find the memorial to Roland Hill,
one of Rugby's great administrators? (Bill
Beaumont couldn't remember, but now it's
something he'll never forget!)

who was the first non-Japanese judo world
champion? (Neither Emlyn nor Bill had a clue!)

Whether you're an active participant in sport or an
armchair supporter and critic, join the duel of wits
in A QUESTION OF SPORT.

Over 600 new questions including full colour photo
section.

BBC/KNIGHT BOOKS

ALSO AVAILABLE IN BBC/KNIGHT:

All these books are available at your local bookshop or newsagent, or can be ordered direc from the publisher. Just tick the titles you want and fill in the form below.

Prices and availability subject to change without notice.

KNIGHT BOOKS, P.O. Box 11, Falmouth, Cornwall.

Please send cheque or postal order, and allow the following for postage an packing:

U.K. – 55p for one book, plus 22p for the second book, and 14p for eac additional book ordered up to a £1.75 maximum.

B.F.P.O. and EIRE – 55p for the first book, plus 22p for the second book and 14p per copy for the next 7 books, 8p per book thereafter.

OTHER OVERSEAS CUSTOMERS – £1.00 for the first book plus 25p pe copy for each additional book.

Name ....

Address ....

....